The Mystery Fancier

may-june '84

$3

The Mystery Fancier

Volume 8, Number 3
May/June 1984

TABLE OF CONTENTS

MYSTERIOUSLY SPEAKING	Page 1
Memories of a Haunted Man By Francis M. Nevins, Jr.	Page 2
Light and Sound by Joseph Hansen By Martha Alderson	Page 12
Who Really Wrote the G-String Murders? By J.R. Christopher	Page 18
Report from Scandinavia By K. Arne Blom	Page 19
On the Onomastics of Sherlock: Replaying the Name Game? By Robert F. Fleissner	Page 21
IT'S ABOUT CRIME By Marvin Lachman	Page 25
REEL MURDERS Movie Reviews by Walter Albert	Page 30
VERDICTS Book Reviews	Page 33
THE DOCUMENTS IN THE CASE Letters	Page 47

The Mystery Fancier
(USPS:428-590)

Steven A. Stilwell, Editor
3004 E. 25th Street
Minneapolis, MN 55406

Guy M. Townsend, Publisher
(and Eminence Grise)
1711 Clifty Drive
Madison, IN 47250

SUBSCRIPTION RATES: Second-class mail, U.S. and Canada, $15.00 per year (6 issues); first-class mail, U.S. and Canada, $18.00; overseas surface mail, $15.00; overseas air mail, $21.00. Overseas subscribers please pay in international money order, check drawn on U.S. bank, or currency; no checks drawn on foreign banks, please. Direct correspondence and manuscripts to the editor; subscription payments and problems should be directed to the publisher.

Single copy price: $3.00
Second-class postage paid at Madison, Indiana
Copyright 1984 by Guy M. Townsend
All rights reserved for contributors
ISSN:0146-3160
Cover by Lari Davidson

    This is always the most difficult part of the magazine for me. Particularly this time. This issue is even later than one would usually expect and I can only ask your forgiveness. It was nearly ready to go almost a month ago (and delayed that long because of some health problems of mine). I had forty-six pages of text done and was going through cleaning up, setting heads, and page numbers, when I tried to delete a file (an article for those not computer literate) that I wasn't going to use. Not only did I delete that particular file but everything else on the disk. Or so I thought since I couldn't get anything to come back up on the screen. Fortunately only my wife was about to hear my sobs (and screams).
    I called the eminence grise to inform him of the problem and to warn him that I was sending him the disk to try and salvage. I might say that he was less than sympathetic. Hysterical would be a better word. Hostile would be another. Though when we started this venture he had used words like "user friendly" and "a forgiving system" in describing the computer and software I would be using, he also said that I should have been making backup files for the work already accomplished. At least he says he said that. I certainly don't remember it.
    To make a long and painful story short, he couldn't do anything so (as per my suggestion) he sent the disk on to **DAPA-EM** official editor aka Emperor of the Universe aka Prince among Emperors aka hacker nonpareil Arthur C. Scott who, by some miracle, was able to salvage the lost magazine. Those with a bent for painful details are invited to write to Art, enclosing a SASE, though I can't guarantee a response. He is heartily sick of this issue. But without him we wouldn't be here today. He now has a lifetime subscription to **TMF**. (GMT take note.) And that's enough about that.
    There's a lot of good things happening out in our field. Reprinting of good old books, first printings of good new books. Joe Gores' first book back in print from The Mysterious Press and Bill Pronzini and John Lutz's collaboration **The Eye** from the same place. I've also heard rumors of a revival of **Black Mask**. Nothing firm on that though. I'll keep you informed and if anyone knows anything for sure, let me know.
    I'm still not getting review copies so I can't tell you about things first hand. Sorry about that. (GMT thinks I took this job for a free computer. Little does he know!)
    Bouchercon is fast approaching and I'll be there. I am **not** the short, balding, red-haired fellow--that's the eminence grise. See you there.

Memories of a Haunted Man

Francis M. Nevins, Jr.

December 12, 1979. A cold brisk day in New York, ideal weather for a walk across Manhattan. I took 50th Street, heading east. When I reached Fifth Avenue my trot slowed to a crawl through a crowd that was sizable even by New York standards. When I asked a traffic cop what was going on he told that the body of Archbishop Fulton Sheen, who had died a few days before, was lying in state in St. Patrick's Cathedral.

If there was a television set in your house in the early 1950s you were almost certain to have heard Sheen's immensely popular Tuesday evening inspirational series **Life Is Worth Living**. You could reject everything the man said, but his magnificent voice could hypnotize you anyway. My crossing the path of Sheen's body that afternoon was a neat ironic touch, because I was on my way to learn more about a man who was a contemporary of Sheen's, and whose habitat, like Sheen's, was New York City, and whose words had the same magical hypnotic power. His message, however, was that life was not worth living at all. I was on my way to have a conversation about Cornell Woolrich.

My appointment was with Lee Wright, the legendary mystery fiction editor, who while at Simon & Schuster had bought Woolrich's earliest suspense novels. She was in her seventies but still semi-active as consultant for Raven House, the now-defunct mystery imprint of Harlequin Books, and it was thanks to her that Raven House reprinted Woolrich's first and perhaps most famous crime novel, **The Bride Wore Black** (1940). Her apartment was on Sutton Place South, a stone's throw form the East River. I recall nothing of what it looked like or how it was furnished. My interest was in the woman who lived in it and her memories of a haunted man.

Nevins: What do you remember about Cornell Woolrich? What did you think of him?

Wright: It was a combination of admiration for his work and a genuine fear that someday he was going to throw me off a roof. He seemed to me such an unstable personality.

N: When did you first meet him, do you remember?

W: Oh, it was many years ago.

N: Did you meet him before he submitted **The Bride Wore Black** to you?

W: Yes, the way I knew many writers.

N: Socially, you mean?

W: You know, through meetings, through.... You know, like you

say, in a social way.
N: Was Woolrich a social kind of person?
W: Not at all. He was a loner and a recluse. He rarely saw anybody, as a matter of fact.
N: Did he go to parties in the evening?
W: I never met him at a party.
N: How did you get to know him then?
W: I met him at some mystery writers' get-together where he wandered in. He said nothing to anybody. And he was a thin wisp of a man.
N: Did you ever meet his mother?
W: She was pretty terrible too. He had an unnatural relationship with his mother ... the true picture of a homosexual's relationship with his mother. A combination of dependence, adoration, hatred, all the things you'd expect.
N: Did he talk about this with other people, or ...?
W: I don't know. He talked about it with me. He had a profound dependence on me, because, I think, he felt that I knew what he was and didn't mind.
N: Was this after you were buying his books?
W: After I began to publish him, yes.
N: You were sort of responsible for his making the transition from being basically a magazine writer to being also a book writer.
W: Well, I did his first book. And I read it very quickly--I always read books very quickly--and called him at once and said it was magnificent. That was **The Bride Wore Black**.
N: Do you know if he submitted it to Simon & Schuster first off, or were you simply somewhere along the line?
W: I don't really know, I never asked him. It seems to me this is an impertinent question.
N: I'm just wondering, because you said you had known him before, whether he ....
W: Yes, I had met him casually, so that I would recognize him if I saw him across the room. I would call him Mr. Woolrich. I wasn't on a first name basis until I began to publish him.
N: I'm sure he was overjoyed when you told him you wanted his novel.
W: He was just in a state of euphoria. I never could convince him that anybody who read that book would have taken it. I didn't want this feeling he had that he owed me so much. You know, these books come along occasionally that anybody would buy who was an editor, or that person shouldn't be an editor. It was like Ira Levin's **A Kiss Before Dying**. You know, I was the first person who saw that. It was a great good book.
N: Did Woolrich then think that **The Bride Wore Black** wasn't all that good? Did he have no confidence in it?
W: I think he had an absolutely unmixed double reaction. One was that every word he wrote was marvelous, magnificent, and shouldn't be changed. And the other was that everything he wrote was terrible, awful, and nobody should read it.
N: A manic-depressive kind of ....
W: Manic-depressive, absolutely. Which led me to believe that he was a little crazy. I still think he was a little crazy. And there was a while when I thought he was dangerous.
N: Physically dangerous?
W: Yeah, I thought he was going to throw me off the roof. We had a penthouse office in the Weber Building on 49th Street and Sixth Avenue and it was an offshoot on ... what floor? The ninth floor.

They had made something just like that, all around the ninth floor. It was like a glass house that they built, and I was afraid he would throw me through the window some day.

N: Did you and he have fights over editing his books, or was it just that he would lose control of himself?

W: he would burst into tears if I didn't say to him: 'Cornell, it was absolutely marvelous.' You had to keep saying that it was absolutely marvelous. But there was no reassuring him. Always: 'Oh. it's no good, it's not good enough for you, I shouldn't even show it to you.' That was step A. Then you would say, 'Well, leave it with me, Cornell, let me be the judge of that, I've never read a word of yours that I didn't think was marvelous. Why should you imagine that i wouldn't like it?' 'Oh, it's no good, it's not good enough.' This would go on for some time and then he would finally leave and go. And I would read it at once and call him. And in the case of **Phantom Lady**, which I saw first--there were other books in between....

N: Right, you bought two for Simon & Schuster. You bought **The Bride Wore Black** and the next one, **The Black Curtain**.

W: And another Black one.

N: **Black Alibi**. Yeah, that's right, you bought three.

W: And **Phantom Lady** was the fourth. And I wanted him to change one paragraph in it which did not ring true. And he said: 'I knew you wouldn't like it, I knew it wasn't good enough for you.' And I said: 'Cornell, I love it, it was wonderful. Just one paragraph. And if you feel strongly about it....'

N: Was this the question--I've heard this from somebody else, I think, that he wanted to leave completely open who the phantom lady was and never explain who she was. Somebody told me he wanted to do it that way.

W: It was something I considered important, but I finally said: 'Cornell, if you feel this strongly about it we'll do it your way. It's your book, you have certain rights, but I wish you'd give it a little thought.' Well, that was the last I saw of him and it was the last I saw of the book. He took it right around the corner to somebody else.

N: Lippincott eventually did it, and of course that created the William Irish name. Do you know anything about that name? This is one of the great mysteries about Woolrich. I don't know if you have a copy of **Nightwebs**, you must have gotten one when it first came out. It was the collection of Woolrich short stories I did. We discovered that there was a real William Irish who was a screenwriter at First National Studios back in the late 1920s when Woolrich was out there, when he had that contract because of that novel he wrote as a boy.

W: It could have been Woolrich.

N: Well, we don't know whether those William Irish screenwriting credits were Woolrich or whether there was a real William Irish whose name he remembered later on, and I was wondering if perhaps you knew.

W: I don't know.

N: That probably is going to be buried in history, that little piece of information. I don't think anybody knows.

W: I simply accepted that it was a made-up name.

N: Of course the style told you instantly. If you knew Woolrich you knew that was the man.

W: Only Woolrich could have written that book.

N: No one could write like him.

W: But I still think **The Bride Wore Black** was a better book. You may think me wrong.

N: Frankly, I agree with most people on that one. I think **Phantom Lady** has much more suspense. Because, you know, in **The Bride Wore Black** you have one person killed, two persons killed, three persons killed....

W: I know, but there's such a vivid imagination in that book.

N: Oh, it's a great book, but I think **Phantom Lady** has more identification, because there's one person whose death you're trying to prevent.

W: I think **Phantom Lady** is more conventional, let's put it that way.

N: Well, that's true, it's the race to save the innocent man from the electric chair. But I don't think anyone has ever written a better book on that theme than **Phantom Lady**.

W: A very good book. But I didn't mind losing it because I was honestly afraid of those wild moods of his when he would burst into tears.

N: Then after he took **Phantom Lady** away from you he just never submitted another book to you? Is that what happened?

W: Apparently he didn't. That was the end of it.

N: I see. Well, then the Black series went to Doubleday. The next one was **The Black Angel**.

W: That wasn't as good as the others.

N: Well, it was **Phantom Lady** with the sexes reversed. And...that's an interesting question. I've talked with other women in the mystery field about this. What did you think about Woolrich's portrayal of women characters?

W: I thought they were very stiff. He was too reverential. He was, the way it was with his mother, too much in awe of women.

N: But the three books you did, none of them had a woman as the viewpoint character the way **The Black Angel** does. I think you never read, as an editor, any of his books told from the long-sustained viewpoint of a woman.

W: No.

N: I was talking with Dorothy Salisbury Davis about this a couple of years ago, and she was unstinting in her praise for the way Woolrich could get into what women were like, more so than any other male writer. I was glad to hear her say that. I thought so too but I don't really have the right to that opinion.

W: Why not?

N: Because I'm the wrong sex. Who as I to say that Woolrich portrays women so well?

W: I don't know, you may know women very well.

N: Maybe so, but it did my heart much good to hear that from a woman like Dorothy Davis.

W: No, I felt he had overwhelming reverence for women, that it was just not good for him.

N: For his own women characters, you mean?

W: That's right. Because it stemmed from his own reaction to women. You know why?

N: I guess it is true that very few of his evil characters are women. Very, very few murderesses in his books.

W: Even in **The Bride Wore Black**?

N: Well, that's a sympathetic murderess.

W: But a really dreadful girl. You know she does some really terrible things, but you....

N: But she does it because they killed or rather she thinks they killed the man she loved. If you're in love you're forgiven everything, that seems to be the rule in Woolrich.

W: He had a reverence for love.
N: Is that because he never had it in his life?
W: But he did have it. He had no excuse. His mother adored him.
N: But I mean aside from his mother. I mean normal relationships with women.
W: He had no normal relationships with women. He couldn't have them.
N: Do you think that's why he portrayed them so intensely, though, in his writing? It was what he couldn't....
W: He wanted it enormously.
N: That comes out, I think, in his writings.
W: He wanted above all things to be a normal man with normal relationships.
N: Why couldn't he be?
W: That depends on what you think makes a homosexual. Was he born that way? I happen to think he was born that way.
N: He didn't talk to you about any of his experiences?
W: No.
N: You know, as a very young man, at about the age of 25, he wrote an autobiographical novel, and I was wondering whether you knew how much of it was fiction. It was called **A Young Man's Heart**
W: Never read it.
N: Well, anyway, it was before he wrote any mysteries at all, this autobiographical thing about a young man growing up in Mexico and his parents separating, the same things that happened to him. I was wondering if he had talked to you about his father?
W: I thought Woolrich was raised in South America.
N: As a boy he was. His father as I understand it was a civil engineer, and his mother was a New York socialite.
W: I never knew what she was, she was like a small mouse.
N: His mother was a small person? I don't know why, but I had always pictured her a large woman. Probably because she dominated Woolrich so much.
W: No. She was fat but small.
N: I see. And of course his parents' marriage broke up when he was a boy.
W: Yes, and he stayed with his mother. He had an absolute adoration for her.
N: He never talked about his father?
W: No.
N: That's interesting, because in that autobiographical novel, which was written so long before you knew him, he seems to like his father quite a bit.
W: Well, I invited him to dinner one night. I felt sorry for him, he kept talking and telling me how.... Every time I saw him he would tell how lonely he was, that nobody loved him, and I would say that he just had to be more outgoing and not be so shy. So this one night I invited him to dinner. My husband was away--oh, yes, I had invited our salesman, Robert Greenan, who has since died. I thought it would entertain Cornell, and it would certainly entertain Robert to meet Cornell. He was a character. Well, they met and we had dinner, and they left at eleven. And Bob had a terrible time protecting himself from Cornell on their way home on the elevated. It almost amounted to a physical attack, because he was so eager to get at Bob.
N: Was that something Cornell did a lot to men?
W: Apparently.
N: No wonder he wasn't too well liked.

W: Some men can be very cruel in rejecting a man.

N: The interesting thing is that there are some incidents dealing with homosexuals in some of his writings. The early ones too. In **Manhattan Love Song**, which is really very close to a suspense novel and brilliantly done, the main character, who's a typical Woolrich loser, at one point falls in love with this strange woman. He desperately needs money to get them both out of the city, and he beats up and robs a homosexual actor who is portrayed by Woolrich with utter contempt.

W: That's what he had for himself, utter contempt. Exactly the right words.

N: You can sense that. If you don't know Woolrich's life it just sounds like the Archie Bunker point of view, but if you do know Woolrich, you know that he's writing about contempt for himself.

W: He was a pitiful figure. Because it was very difficult to like him.

N: That;s pretty much what everyone has said, that he was impossible to deal with on a personal level.

W: When he moved to that hotel, a very nice hotel....

N: The Sheraton Russell? I know he was there for a while. He was in two or three at different times. I think the Sheraton Russell was the one where he died. I forget the names of the others.

W: He called me. I hadn't seen him for a long time and he called me one day and asked could I please come up and see him, he was very lonely and very alone, an he badly needed to see someone whom he respected and liked. So I went up. We had teas together. And from then on, about once a month, I made it my business to call on him and visit him.

N: Even after you weren't publishing him any more.?

W: Oh, long after. But I was sorry for him. He was so alone and so lonely and his legs had given out on him, he was sort of bedridden.

N: This was after his mother died?

W: No, she was still alive.

N: She died in 1958, I think, 1957 or 58.

W: This must have been about 1952.

N: He must have stopped writing by then.

W: Yes, he had stopped writing. And he never wanted to talk about money. I think he was afraid that if he talked about it somebody would try to take it away from him.

N: There was money in his family, wasn't there?

W: Well, he had made a great deal of money from the first moment he wrote. **Children of the Ritz**, was it?

N: Yes, he won a big prize for that.

W: He won a prize, that started it.

N: But I've got his financial records, I work for his estate. And he was making good money, for the time it was quite good money, but nothing spectacular, nothing in the million or half million dollar range. But I was wondering whether his mother....

W: He left, it must have been over a million.

N: It was just around a million, slightly under. But that was not in cash, I gather that was largely what he got when his mother died. I'm not really certain. And , of course, he left all the literary properties to the trust fund for Columbia University. Was he worried about money?

W: Always worried a little.

N: He never really spent much. I was told the only thing he ever bought was booze.

W: A lot of that. But he worried about it. He was a confirmed miser.

N: When you look at the few pictures of him that exist you think he never wore a decent suit in his life. And I'm sure he didn't eat much, considering how thin he was.

W: Well, big drinkers are very rarely big eaters.

N: I was told he could go through a bottle a day like nothing.

W: I would say two bottles.

N: Didn't his mother try to stop him from drinking like that?

W: I don't know what she did when they were alone.

N: You'd think she could have laid down the law to him, if she really had so much control over him and if she wanted him to stop drinking, or whatever.

W: Well, I suppose she did and she didn't. Nobody could control him all the time.

N: And you sort of kept seeing him a little at a time.

W: There was a period when I didn't see him for a long time, and then he called me.

N: Did you ever try to get him to write books again?

W: No.

N: He had pretty much dried up, I guess, by then?

W: I felt that if he wanted to write books he would. There was no point in my nudging him. And I didn't want to have anything to do with him professionally. Because I was scared of him. He was so....

N: Everyone, of course, has told me different stories about Woolrich and how difficult he was. You know, it's almost as if there's a consensus. Everyone loves his work beyond words and no one could stand him as a person.

W: That about sums it up. If you saw him or paid attention to him, you had to respect him as a writer.

N: How he could put those words together!

W: How those words came out of this skinny rat of a man!

N: If you could see the picture Mike Avallone gave me for the back of the jacket of **Nightwebs**, he looks like the kind of Bowery bum who'd stop you for a dime on the street. One of the greatest writers that ever lived.

W: He had red eyes.

N: You mean bloodshot eyes?

W: I don't know if they were bloodshot, they were just red.

N: Unusual color. What happened then as far as you and Woolrich were concerned? You drifted off?

W: Drifted off, yes.

N: Have you heard about his having a leg amputated and all that? So sad. I was a law student and living about a mile or so from where he lived during his last years, but I didn't know him. From what I knew about him I didn't think he would welcome a strange young law student coming up to him and telling him how much he....

W: He would have loved it.

N: I wish I'd known that. I was a timid law student in those days. Today I would do it, the way I feel about things. But I mean, who was I?...It's a shame.

W: He was very alone. He had an aunt.

N: The one who lived in Jersey?

W: Yeah.

N: He didn't leave her anything, though, when he died. He left it all to Columbia. That's how I got into the Woolrich picture, when he did that. Because the Chase Manhattan Bank people had no idea what it was they were administering. He kept no records his life long. He didn't have any file of what he had written, what the status of it was, what rights he had sold—nothing.

W: You had to collect this out of thin air?

N: Well, I knew something of what he'd written and, more important, I knew two men, Harold Knott and William Thailing, my collaborators on **Nightwebs**, who knew a lot more than I did, who had been Woolrich aficionados since the 1940s.

W: That was a piece of luck.

N: Yeah. The three of us put together a complete checklist of everything he had written and then with that as a basis we could go into the Copyright Office records and find out what had been renewed, what had not been renewed, what was of questionable legal status. And I would up doing a very thick book on the legal status of every scrap Woolrich ever wrote. That's the basis of every deal the estate has made or will make until the last copyright runs out.

W: So that's the way you came into the picture?

N: I owed the man so much. I cared for his writing that much.

W: Very few people would have had the sense of responsibility toward writing.

N: Well, Woolrich was responsible for a lot of my success too. It was largely through my activity with the Woolrich estate that got me into the field of copyright law, which I now teach, thanks largely to working on the Woolrich estate. That gave me the practical experience and the impetus. And then when I got my teaching job, I started a copyright course at the law school, which hadn't had one before. So one thing leads to another and I've been compensated many times over for the work I've put in for the estate of Woolrich.

W: But the thing that motivated you to start was a very devoted and unselfish impulse which I admire. it's almost a responsibility toward the artist.

N: I really don't know how to put it into words. I'll never regret that I did it.

W: It worked out very well for you.

N: For everyone involved. I did very well with **Nightwebs** and we got a lot of stories current again.

W: It doesn't always happen that way. What starts as a purely unselfish, almost noble pursuit, pays off.

At this point the tape ran out and it was time to switch to the other side. While I was doing this, our conversation somehow moved away from Woolrich and in the direction of other crime writers with whom Lee Wright had worked. After about fifteen or twenty minutes the poet of the shadows came back.

W: We've come a long way from Woolrich, but there's very little more I can tell you about him.

N: You've told me plenty. I remember when I first met you at Bill Pronzini's house, about five years ago, you seemed from what you said to dislike Woolrich. And I guess I had never really met anybody else.... I had interviewed almost everybody else that know him at all well, and they all felt sorry for him but none of them would say that they disliked him. I think you said he cause his own problems, and things of that sort.

W: Yes, of course.

N: And that was a different view of Woolrich completely.

W: It was very difficult to like him.

N: I guess a lot of people felt like that but not too many really wanted to say it, because they felt sorry for him.

W: That's right. I felt sorry for him but that doesn't constitute liking him. In fact, it's frequently a basis for disliking somebody, because he's evoking a reaction from you that you don't want to give him.

N: In his writing he seems to be calling out desperately for someone to care for him.

W: Yes, he did. He actually did call out, as you know.

N: Nobody else can do that. I mean, it's not something you can fake, it's not something you can learn how to do technically. And I think it's just not worth it to have that talent, because it means that your life is an utter wretchedness from first breath to last.

W: Yes, I would say that Cornell led a very miserable life.

N: And that's why there will never be another suspense writer like Woolrich, because you have to pay for it.

W: You pay for it the rest of your life.

N: That's right. And that's why everybody else in the field is just a technician—except Woolrich. Woolrich lived it in his bones. It wasn't just technique.

W: Well, there are some other people who are very good. Hilda Lawrence.

N: I've read some of hers.

W: I thought she wrote first-rate suspense.

N: There are a lot of good suspense writers, but you never get the feeling with anybody else that this is their guts and their blood and their bones that you get with Woolrich.

W: Well, it was.

N: The only thing I know that is remotely similar is Hitchcock.

W: The total dedication, the total immersion in what he's doing.

N: I think in Hitchcock too, you know, it's buried so deep down even he can't dredge it up. And I think that comes out of his own bones and blood too. He talks about it in very oblique ways now and then, the same story he tells over and over about how his father had him locked up as a little boy. And of course he talks about the Jesuits beating him and a few things like that. I think all those terrors in his films--they're real too. They're not things that a skillful writer imagines. He and Woolrich are two of a kind.

W: And yet Hitchcock can be very funny.

N: Woolrich really couldn't be.

W: Never. He had no sense of humor at all.

N: A couple of times he tried to write humorous stories. There's one, which I think is a disaster, which had been reprinted in several anthologies. It's a horrible story, an absolutely awful thing called "Wild Bill Hiccup". I can't even recall what it's about. It's supposed to be funny. But it's not, though it's very short and I think that's why it's been reprinted, because most of stories are so long.

W: Probably.

N: Did you go to the movies that were based on Woolrich as you were working with him and seeing him in the forties? He seemed to be a real movie buff, you'll find a lot of movie references if you look at those stories.

W: He did like movies.

N: One thing I've noticed. If you know exactly when a Woolrich story was published, say in a pulp magazine, and if you think back a year or six months prior to that, you can think of some fairly well-known movie with something in it similar to that story which just seems to have sparked him. Some motif in a picture. Movies really affected him, I think. They were a big part of what moved him to write.

W: It was something he could do alone. And he was almost always alone. Cornell had no playmates.

N: There was no one he could talk to even about how he wrote the way he did. It makes you shudder to think what a wretched life it was.

W: What I got from Cornell was this absolute idiot adoration, a combination of that and a sense of awe. He was afraid of me. I was not his idea of what a woman should be.

N: Because you were a businesswoman?

W: Probably, and also because I'm very firm, and I have a firm voice.

N: And yet he has women do very aggressive, active things. Otto Penzler did a whole collection of stories, which I helped him edit, about Woolrich women characters, in which they are the protagonists. They're rich and they're poor and they're young and they're old and they're in all walks of life, but they control their stories. He must on some level have admired women of that sort.

W: Yes, I think his mother was a very forceful person underneath the mouselike exterior. But I don't even have a mouselike exterior!

N: I never though of Woolrich's mother as a mouselike person. I don't know if you know this, but he did write an autobiography—though he never finished it. He had four unfinished books when he died. I have copies of them all, thanks to the estate. Two unfinished novels and a third almost finished. Did you ever see it? He worked this book for ten years or more, and except for one scene it's finished. Apparently it was rejected by everybody in New York back in the early Sixties. I think it was the best thing he wrote in the last twenty years of his life, and after his death we still haven't been able to find a publisher for it.

W: Has it any detection?

N: I'll tell you the story line. It's a combination of themes from several of the earlier books, including **The Bride Wore Black** and **Phantom Lady**. The beginning of the book is missing, the first twenty pages, but I think it's a moire poignant book because it starts in the middle that way. You get the impression...

At this point, much like the Woolrich manuscript I was describing, my tape just stopped. It was far from the end of our conversation however; we kept talking for at least another half hour, without the benefit of technology and without any more Woolrich. That was a golden afternoon for me, and I'm deeply grateful to Ms. Wright for sharing with me her memories and perceptions of the haunted, wretched man whom she first introduced to the world as a suspense novelist.

Light and Sound by Joseph Henson

Martha Alderson

Suspense stories with private eyes are usually propelled chiefly by strong, terse dialogue. In his autobiographical **The Pulp Jungle**, Frank Gruber describes the shift in writing style of crime fiction credited to Raymond Chandler, Dashiell Hammett, and the **Black Mask** "School of Writing" of the early 1930's:

> In the United States, writers were trying to inject more realism into their stories. They stripped them of verbiage, blue-penciled the descriptive passages, kept their stories moving. The characters became strong, silent men. The stories became more violent, the prose became sparser."[1]

Fans of crime fiction have learned in these 50 years to skim the descriptive fillers for minimal details because the dialogue is so often the story.

Joseph Hansen's mystery novels feature a private eye, fast pace, spicy dialogue, strong (although not usually silent) men, and enough violence to qualify as realism; but his running prose is not minimal and is not superfluous. The imagery is too rich to miss. Besides giving factual data of time and place, long chapter introductions and many other narrative sequences are deliciously descriptive of weather, topography, and people.

In one of his non-mystery novels, Hansen suggests that "The U.S. tilts. Everything not too square to roll ends up on the West Coast."[2] All of Hansen's mystery novels, in the Dave Brandstetter series[3] and the non-series suspense novel[4] take place in traditional private-eye country, southern California, which is where Hansen himself lives. Whether or not the rest of us believe we are too square to roll to the exciting West, we must believe Hansen loves California.

Hansen shows his affection for the coastal environment through many scenes, like this one, personifying the ocean that "wrote white scribbles to itself on a blue slate under a wide smile of sky. The surf lipped pale sand beyond a stagger of red dune fences". (**Troublemaker**, 19)

His descriptions remind all readers of the special nature of California geology that is both ocean and desert. Not far from waves and beaches are not only lushly covered mountains but also craggy land and lovely plants of an arid climate. Hansen includes "the wild flowers--lupines, poppies--blue and gold, that carpeted the desert for miles around all directions these few weeks in February" (**Gravedigger**, 90). He also describes the stately and dangerous canyons that change so dramatically when drought is punctuated by rain.

> Yucca Canyon was even wilder and more empty than he had thought last night. At first, the road wound up from the coast among broad, low foothills, then entered a narrow pass, where it edged an arroyo overhung with the leafless, white, and twisting arms of big sycamores. Rain runoff plunged down the arroyo, foaming muddily, tumbling boulders with its force. (**Gravedigger**, 99)

> The spur of Torcido Canyon to which Melvil pointed him would have been easy to miss. Its road was a narrow strip of blacktop that the rain had damaged. It followed a crooked creek along the bottom of a canyon whose walls went up steeply, covered in dry brush showing new tips of green, with occasional clumps of live oak and outcrops of rock. The ridges were high above. The creek ran rough and swollen among boulders and twisted white sycamores hung with scraps of yellow leaf. (**Nightwork**, 150)

Frequently Hansen contrasts the sensual pleasures of nature with the ugly, nevertheless colorful, effects of poverty and despair. These passages create as much an appreciation of a simple beauty as sadness at the unfortunate conditions. He has the narrator of **Backtrack** tell that:

> Los Angeles has a lot of shabby corners. Joanna Payne Antiques was in one of them. Past the flat-roofed grubby one-story buildings with their scabby signs, you could see, if you looked, green mountains, sky that was a good color on this particular day, and treetops in back of some places. But there was a lot of hopelessness to the grimy windows where the displays faded in the sun, the trash in the gutters, the cracked sidewalks, the fat Mexican grandmothers hobbling past with broken coasterwagons, the sick old black men sitting bony in doorways of climb-the-stairs hotels. (76)

Dave Brandstetter is very much aware of the contrasts as he drives:

> down twisting streets past old apartment courts where doors were enameled bright colors and sported new brass knockers, where windbells hung in trees, and where lissome young men in swim trunks clipped hedges or soaped down little sports cars at the curbs. Then, another level lower, he passed rickety wood-framed houses in need of paint, where radios blared mariachi music through rusty window screens, and little brown Mexican kids swarmed in yards where no grass grew. (**Skinflick**, 11)

Landscape that shouts of its glory also brings awareness of the quiet loneliness of the inhabitants. Dave considers the scene as he drives along in his small, uncomfortable Triumph seeking facts and justice.

> It was lonely country lifting gently toward ragged mountains through low hills velvet with new green from

winter rains, hills strewn with white rocks and clumps of
brush, and slashed here and there by ravines dark with big
live-oaks. An eight-lane freeway had brought him into the
hills from the seacoast, forty clean, sleek miles of new
cement leading God knew where, nobody driving it but
him, under low-hanging clouds, dark and tattered,
spattering the windshield with squall of rain one minute,
the next minute letting shafts of sunlight through.
(**Gravedigger**, 61)

In the seven mysteries in the Dave Brandstetter series and the one non-Brandstetter suspense novel, Hansen liberally sprinkles references that make the reader feel the heat, smell the rain, or cough in the fog. Manzanita, eucalyptus, bougainvillea; goats and burros; Spanish Mission architecture, commercially developed or abandoned fishing piers, canneries; dunes, canyons, arroyos; suburbs and slums--all speak with loving, insightful clarity of southern California.

The Hansen sound track is as impressive as the visual effects. It is created, of course, by the ocean, the wind, the rain, and other forces of nature and humanity. In **Nightwork**, "Gifford's laugh was a crackle of dead leaves" (96). In **Death**, a century-old waterwheel is described as having "Wooden stutter like children running down a hall at the end of school. Grudging axle thud like the heartbeat of a strong old man." (15)

As Brandstetter keeps a lonely vigil on the side of the road, he could not actually see the ocean. "But he could feel it thud against the cliff, and hear it hiss among the rocks when it pulled back to strike again." (**Gravedigger**, 118)

The hissing ocean, crackling laughs, and sputtering water wheels heighten the tension by creating a realistic and haunting atmosphere.

In a touch of humor in the sound track, Hansen carelessly uses the same description in two books. In both **Death Claims** (23) and **Skinflick** (2), Dave Brandstetter rings a doorbell that plays the first four notes of the old gospel hymn "Love Lifted Me". Although it is an effective sound effect, readers could wish he had varied the tune.

In addition to descriptions of the light and sound of nature, there are clear and lovely images of people. All the Hansen mystery novels have a variety of characters from a cross section of humanity. There are the rich, the poor, the plain and simple, the sleazy and smooth, jet setters, rednecks, and naturally for the Western settings, the cowboys (urban mostly). Each appears with marvelous detail.

Dave Brandstetter himself is an insurance investigator for death claims. In the novel **Death Claims**, a visiting evangelist is described as "a man with a mane of straw-colored hair and a face like a new plow blade". (24) When a youth appears from the bedroom of one of the suspects, Dave observes that "there was nothing saintly in his brown eyes. There was almost nothing at all". (21) One character's skin "was webbed like a winter-morning window in snow country". (30) Another's is "brown and creased as an old harness". (28)

Dave reminisces frequently about his childhood and about his father's nine (sequential) wives. Dave remembers the first as a "bewildered girl who was my lost mother's replacement, a breasty, wide-eyed blonde child who lived in a pink kimono stitched with a pale-green dragon and in a haze of Turkish cigarette smoke". (**Death**, 88)

An example of a short portrait that cuts to the essence of the character is the description of a business executive whose "clothes, suntan, manner, car, didn't belong to the image of a man who took the office home with him". (**Skinflick**, 40) It is said of a character in another novel that "what showed his age were his eyes, hard, bright, and wary—eyes that had seen too much and doubted most of it". (**Man**, 64)

A short piece of dialogue from **Troublemaker** between a 60-year old woman and her estranged husband whom she has not seen for many years says a great deal very simply:

> "Dear God—what's happened to you?"
> "Happened?" he said. "I'm sixty-five years old."
(66)

These colorful portrayals of various types of characters are in some ways a result of the Hansen theme of social justice. The fact that Dave Brandstetter is gay says much about the social themes. Descriptions of Dave Brandstetter always point out that he is ruggedly handsome, sophisticated, strong, and thoughtful. By precept and example Dave spreads the word throughout southern California that gay types are not always types at all, that it is not good for physical or mental health to keep homosexual behavior "in the closet", (especially while exploiting other sexual behavior), and that stereotyping of any kind is counterproductive.

Hansen targets many kinds of bigotry. Religious hypocrisy is evident in several of the mysteries, and religious hypocrisy, like all hypocrisy, has a negative effect on people. But, religious fanaticism in these novels isn't in itself evil--it's a fact of some people's lives, often harmful but not necessarily wrong. Most characters are caucasian, but important major characters are black, Spanish, and Oriental. Although Dave Brandstetter is in his fiftie's and depressed about aging, the effect of many descriptions and events involving age fight against the bias of ageism. In fact, Brandstetter's possibly permanent lover (still, as of the 1984 **Nightwork**) is a young black man, Cecil Harris, who is some thirty years younger than Dave. (Cecil is, of course, a wonderful human being, bright, and kind.)

A touching portrayal in the first novel **Fadeout** is of a cerebral palsy victim. Dave finds the youth insightful as well as pleasant company. Dave comes to understand how worthwhile it is to spend the time and energy required to talk with Buddy Mundy whose "smile was better than the human average". (74)

A main character in **Gravedigger** is a Juilliard student, a musical genius who has a severe speech impediment, severe enough that most people at first cannot understand him at all. After a few encounters, Dave agrees with one of Lyle Westover's friends that "you don't notice that, ...not after a while. It doesn't matter". (40)

In interesting detail Hansen presents all of these people who are not "average" with great dignity. Hansen's books would certainly meet any publisher's guidelines for bias-free writing.

Another group of effective descriptions are of tourists. hansen seems to be amused by tourists in California. He especially comments on Midwesterners who he must think embody the essence of the tourist. These, for example:

> Along a stretch of wide West Santa Monica Boulevard where the city criminal code didn't reach, signs, red, blue, yellow, flashed names at the rental cars of tourists that crawled past, bumper to bumper, while the Iowans inside, eyes circled by white from desert sunglasses, marveled. (**Troublemaker**, 139)

> Across the [street] lay the park with the little lake, the ducks in the rushes, the muggers in the bushes, the sunburned tourists rowing battered little skiffs and peering through Instamatics at the glass skyscrapers beyond the tops of the palms. (**Skinflick**, 11)

> Pinatas hung from the old black rafters.... With flat tissue-paper eyes, they watched Indianans in Bermuda shorts and sundresses inch their way along the narrow bricked lanes.... (**Skinflick**, 116)

It must be noted that some of Hansen's metaphors and similes read like parodies of the one-liners of older hard-boiled fiction masters. The very best is this one: "...she gave him a grin that couldn't have been friendlier if she'd had teeth." (**Fadeout**, 134) Another that works is a description of the expression on the face of a corpse in a police photo: "He looked as if the last thing he could imagine was being dead." (**Gravedigger**, 25) And this: "The trouble with life was, nobody ever got enough rehearsal." (**Skinflick**, 108)

A few of these parodies are not so successful, in fact are somewhat strained. Two of the worst are from the suspenseful **Backtrack**. **Backtrack** is not a Brandstetter book and is told in the first person by a brash 18-year old, which may account for the strain. The narrator comments that a man's "shirt collar was so high that when he talked, you expected a ten second delay for the sound to reach you".(60) About a woman he says, "Her smile had more creases than an origami instruction book". (38)

But most Hansen comparisons are fresh and clever:

> Gulls fell like scraps of china from a blue tablecloth sky. (**Backtrack**, 37)
> The carpet...was thick enough to make it dangerous for anybody with weak ankles. (**Skinflick**, 12)
> She...had starved herself to keep her figure right for a bikini and had almost managed it. (**Man**, 66)
> The voice...was raspy and defeated. Like a fan's who's cheered fourteen innings for the team that lost. (**Death**, 92)

Hansen repeatedly uses one curious image, an ashtray. In an **Ellery Queen's Mystery Magazine** interview Hansen explained one of his ashtray descriptions as simply a writing style:

> Hansen:...As to that ashtray--I think if you're going to use a prop, you ought to show what it looks like. This adds conviction to a scene for the reader, takes him there.[5]

The interviewer did not point out that there are in fact so many descriptions of ashtrays that they must be more important than just a touch of realism as Hansen says. Here are a few examples: "...the mechanism of a lighter glinted in a burl of polished wood." (**Fadeout**, 4); "The ashtray was black Mexican pottery." (**Fadeout**, 5); "The ashtray was a rough stone mortar." (**Fadeout**, 21); "The tiny counter ashtray was yellow plastic. It looked flammable." (**Fadeout**, 57); "A pair of china parakeets billed on the frilly rim of an ashtray...." (**Death**, 4); "The ashtray was thick pewter stamped with a coat of arms. Hound and Hooded hawk." (**Death**, 39); "The ashtray was in the shape of a ship's helm, with a shallow bowl of amber glass set into it." (**Skinflick**, 96).

In addition to these, we read about a "hammered copper ashtray" (**Death**, 79), an "abalone-shell ashtray" (**Man**, 63), a "brown pottery ashtray" (**Gravedigger**, 10), a "terra-cotta ashtray glazed blue inside" (**Gravedigger**, 68), and a "fluted pink china ashtray" (**Nightwork**, 89). The only safe conclusion is that the Hansen characters smoke a lot! In contrast to the many references to Dave's slim, steel lighter—surely a symbol of his masculinity as well as a reminder of his father and his youth—the ashtrays do not have any clear symbolic significance. If they have any special meaning, it is either too obvious or too hidden. Quite likely they are merely, or importantly, a signature in a Hansen book.

Joseph Hansen's mysteries have much to recommend them. One can hunt for ashtrays, enjoy the suspense, admire the characters, and be comforted by themes of justice and civil liberties. An added pleasure is the fact that the lighting, sound, and other images are stunning. Those who are used to skimming the descriptive details in private-eye novels should change their habits by reading Joseph Hansen slowly and then should consider giving him an award for special effects.

NOTES

1. Gruber, Frank. **The Pulp Jungle**. Los Angeles: Sherbourne Press, Inc., 1967, p.145.
2. Hansen, Joseph. **A Smile in His Lifetime**. New York: Holt, Rinehart and Winston, 1981, p. 57.
3. **Fadeout**. Holt, Rinehart and Winston, Holt, 1980, paper. **Death Claims**. Holt, 1980, paper. **Troublemaker**, Holt, 1981, paper. **The Man Everybody was Afraid Of**. Holt, 1981, paper. **Skinflick**, Holt, 1980, paper. **Gravedigger**, Holt, 1982. **Nightwork**, Holt, 1984.
4. **Backtrack**, The Countryman Press, 1982.
5. **Ellery Queen's Mystery Magazine**, September 1983. 82:4:71.

Who Really Wrote The G-String Murders?

J. R. Christopher

Julian Symons, in **Mortal Consequences** (1970), gives a paragraph to Gypsy Rose Lee's two mystery novels, **The G-String Murders** (1941), "a cheerfully ribald book", and **Mother Finds a Body** (1942) on "the whole [a] much inferior" volume. He seems to know nothing of the books being ghostwritten, although the phrasing is ambiguous: "Two detective stories appeared under the professional name of striptease artist Gypsy Rose Lee, whose real name was Rose Louise Horvick (1914-1970)." Jacques Barzun and Wendell Hertig Taylor, in **A Catalogue of Crime** (1971), know nothing of a ghost writer.

But five years later, in **Encyclopedia of Mystery and Detection**, edited by Chris Steinbrunner and Otto Penzler, under **Gypsy Rose Lee** there is simply a cross-reference to **Craig Rice**, where one reads that Rice was "publicity agent for Gypsy Rose Lee and published two successful murder mysteries, **The G-String Murders** (1941) and **Mother Finds a Body** (1942), under that famous burlesque dancer's name." This has become the standard information, as one can find by checking **Gypsy Rose Lee** in Allen J. Hubin's **Crime Fiction, 1749-1980: A Comprehensive Bibliography** (1984).

Probably Craig Rice did write the books--they seem to have her liveliness. But I would like to complicate the attribution, for I have run across another statement--one in a book which I expect many mystery readers have not read. In Humphrey Carpenter's **W. H. Auden: A Biography** (19810, Auden's life, following October, 1940, is described; he was living in a rather bohemian brownstone owned by George Davis at 7 Middagh Street, Brooklyn Heights, New York City. Carpenter writes:

> Another resident--or more probably a regular visitor--was a friend of George Davis, whose book **The G-String Murders** he was ghost writing, the striptease artist Gypsy Rose Lee.

Is it possible that this is right, and George Davis, not Craig Rice, wrote the book--the better of the two novels according to Symons? Hubin does not list any novels by an American George Davis about this period, so he does not seem a probable ghost. Still, that is certainly what Carpenter says.

Neither Steinbrunner and Penzler on the one hand nor Carpenter on the other give their sources of information. But I have one suggestion which may allow for a way out. Carpenter identifies Davis as "a New York Literary editor". He may just have been the person

(Continued on page 20)

A Report from Scandinavia

K. Arne Blom

When I see it in print, I discover that somewhere the pun was lost. In my last report I wrote about the brilliant hardboiled mysteries by the Danish writer Dan Turell and called them Op Blues. It should have been cOPenhagen BLUES. That's better.

The last week in August is a good week over here. **Hill Street Blues** will be back on TV. We are like 50 episodes behind, but the main thing is that it will be back on the air again. Would you believe it, some idiot of a genius who is responsible for what is shown claimed a year ago the HSB wasn't good enough to be shown in Sweden. Well, we formed kind of a pressure group—I guess we were four or five—and forced it back. Maybe one the reasons it can be shown on Swedish TV again is the fact, that on Danish TV they understand that it is one of the finest of its kind ever made, and they are showing it and laughing at that idiot in Sweden. They give us **Remington Steele** and **Magnum** and **Hart to Hart** and think them good, and then say that **Hill Street Blues**.... Well....

Speaking about TV and mysteries—one of the the best—possibly the best—series made in Scandinavia was one called **En by i provinsen** (A Small Town in the Countryside) and focused on a small police force and their struggle to deal with crimes and problems. In Denmark they know what is good—they make good TV series and they show the best (from our point of view) foreign ones. And, luckily enough, I live where we are able to watch Danish television.

Have you ever read a good German mystery? I haven't. The strange thing is that the Germans are somewhat the European champions when it comes to TV mysteries. Three series are outstanding: **Keller** (about a policeman and his men), **Der Alte** (The Old Man-about another policeman and his doings) and **Tatort** (Big City-which comes close to being a kind of German 87th Precinct series). The German series are different, they are realistic and they portray people, crimes and milieus in a way that is real, believable, touching, and gripping. Do you get any German series over there? Or the French ones? They are not as good as the German ones, but they did the best Maigret series; and when they worked with William Irish's short stories, they turned those masterpieces into masterful TV stories. They did a long series and one enjoyed every minute of it. It is not only the English that are capable of producing good TV mystery series. They are good at it, but not all that comes out of there is memorable.

Speaking about France, it is rumoured that the next Crime Writers International Congress will take place in Versailles. The first one was in 1975 in London, the second in New York in 1978, the third in Stockholm in 1981, and the fourth should have been arranged in Los Angeles this year. It is next year in Versailles instead. And then, according to good friends in England, it will be LOndon again in 1988. There is something magic about that. I bet the English wouldn't miss it. Why? Well, think. What happened in 1888? Yes, you're right. They called him Jack the Ripper. 100 years ago.

I was quite surprised when I learned that **The Mystery Fancier** and **The Armchair Detective** were printed and sold in so few copies. There are two similar magazines existing in Sweden: **Jury** and **DAST**. The circulation of **TMF** is less than a thousand copies, and I don't know about **TAD** right now, but it is not much over 2000, if that. I heard a figure some three years ago saying 1600. **Jury** has got 2000 subscribers and **DAST** well over a thousand. The amazing thing is that Sweden is a so much smaller country than the U.S.--and that so few people over here are subscribing and reading **TMF** and **TAD**. Where are the big masses of readers in the U.S.? And then there is a fine magazine published in Denmark. It is called **Pinkerton** and is edited by Bjarne Nielsen, who is also a secondhand bookseller (of mysteries) and starting this fall will also be a publisher of mysteries and books about mysteries.

The mystery is still a big thing in Scandinavia.

(Continued from page 18): who arranged for Rice to write the book (although the S&P account of her being Lee's publicity agent is against that), or he may have marketed the book for Lee and Rice, and the story got distorted by the time it reached Carpenter. The uncertainty about whether or not Lee was living in the brownstone suggests some weakness in Carpenter's source.

However, I think it appropriate that in the hidden world of ghost-writing some confusion, some doubt, continue to exist. (I also wonder who ghostwrote Lee's later autobiography, **Gypsy**? But, by my principles, maybe I shouldn't ask.)

(Continued from page 24:) demand of each other. Unfortunately, that's the one thing the cosmic-toadstoolers are short of. Ockham's Razor disposes neatly of most psychic and paranormal claims, and those that survive that test are supported by nothing more than wishful thinking.

I'm looking forward to a tooth-and-nail discussion of the subject with you at Bouchercon, Jon--that is, if I don't spontaneously combust before then and am not abducted by flying-saucer men on my way up to Chicago.

The Onomastics of Sherlock

Robert F. Fleissner

The Sign of the Four is replete with recondite allusions to etymology and the origin of the detective's name. A study in what is called the science of deduction (albeit more concerned scientifically with induction), the first chapter starts off with a reference to Holmes' interest in "the most abstruse cryptogram", his "genius for minitiae", wordplay on the name **Sherlock** in various ways, and then ends with a curious statement of misdirection: "I have no recollection of the name". Although the name in question is that of Mary Morstan, such a pronouncement after so many hints on onomastic matters have preceded it is indeed a puzzle. Let us consider the nomenclatural points now in detail.

The first clue to the name play is found in the cryptogrammatic allusion; we are led to wonder whether Sherlock's own name may have had that meaning for Doyle, and some evidence exists to that effect, but since onomastics is concerned not merely with the author's own intent but with what others have made of unconscious reverberations, let us keep an open mind. The ultimate significance of **Sherlock Holmes** may well be more mythic than anything else. However we formulate our quest, the fact that Conan Doyle himself claimed that he borrowed Sherlock's name from a player of a game, Cricket, provides a precedent for the name game. For did he his "gamesmanship" seriously?

Shortly we hear Sherlock's off-hand remark to Watson, "Ah, that is good luck." After a few short sentences, he speaks of a "shocking" habit. It is altogether clear that the connotations of **luck** and **shock** would have combined in Doyle's unconscious to generate an association with **Sherlock**. They certainly have, I hastily submit, for Sherlockians since then, for they have led to various pastiche names, notably **Sheerluck Jones**, considered a "refreshing and capital travesty of the Doyle/Gillette monodrama", **Sherlock Holmes**.[1] Independently, I have come across another recent travesty with the sleuth designated **Sheerluck Holds**.[2] There must be many more. Indeed, at a recent Sherlockian conference I co-directed, one of the participants automatically thought of "sheer luck" as a parody of **Sherlock**.[3] "The luck of the Irish", we might say, remembering that Doyle had an Irish heritage. Let us keep the memory of his name also green.

As for **shock**, surely we must think of **Schlock Homes**, the name of whom invites the verdict that much pastiche and parody, mostly the latter, has taken the form of **Schlock** (or **Kitsch**) art. The numerous examples in the recent compendium **Sherlock Holmes in America** provide much evidence of this tendency. But of course the connotations of **schlock** would have been too late for Doyle himself.

More relevant historically would be Jon L. Lellenberg's comment that too many publishers of take-offs today "seem to believe that a story must have some **shock** value or a gimmick to make it attractive to the masses".[4] This the connotations of **shock** too are built onto Sherlock's name, at least for the uninitiated. The true reader of the CAnon would see that the detective was much too reserved to ponder such a meaning in his own cognomen. Indeed, the very passage cited from **The Sign of the Four** containing the word "shocking" indicates as much. But it would appear that unconsciously Doyle anticipated what would happen with some modern trends.

One other connotation of Sherlock's name is deployed in the opening chapter: it is found in the paragraph about the key-hole. Although ostensibly about a lock made by a drunk (a rather far-fetched ploy to modern sleuths), the very notion of a **lock** being brought up has its hidden implications again. Is Sherlock so called because of his ability to **lock** up criminals? This assumption is hardly new with me (having been advanced, for example, by our family handyman), though the transformation of **Sher-** into **sure** (for him to "sure lock" them up) is more comical than cogent. Not to be forgotten is that the **-lock** suffix could also relate to a possible connection with the name **Shylock**, both Shakespeare's Jew and Sherlock being men of justice in their own right, even being "shysters" to the extent that they take the law into their own hands at times to gain their ends.[5] Owen Dudley Edwards' recent book which emphasizes the Scottish background of Doyle, even to the extent of claiming that London settings in the stories had their antecedents in Edinburgh, makes an issue of **Sherlock** being the name of the dumbest boy in Doyle's class there.[6] Perhaps so, but a connection of the familiar Scottish word **loch** (as in watery "Loch Lohman") may also be present, just as easily. Compare Sherrin**ford**.

Edwards' views have been criticized in the **TLS** review on the grounds Conan Doyle had other acknowledged sources for his names;[7] indeed, he knew a cricketplayer named Sherlock, and since the author was such a sportsman (having, for instance, introduced skiing into Switzerland), such an etymology may appear more likely than a remembrance of such an old school chum. The argument, however, is that Conan Doyle would scarcely have admitted getting the name of the brightest of detectives from a flunky, so to speak, even if he originally had a private joke in mind. That he would not have been against such an odd reversal might been seen in his naming his arch-villain with an Irish surname when he himself was of Irish descent. He simply was not that sensitive about his own heritage. For that matter, as has been pointed out, **Sherlock** may derive, in part, from Sherlockstown in Ireland.[8] Why not?

Steven Lauria has recently summed up the etymological studies on "The Name Sherlock" by pointing to Baring-Gould's belief that the Master's father "insisted that the boy should be named William Sherlock, for [he] had long been an admirer of that seventeenth-century theologian and author";[9] Lauria himself, however, favors an association with the shearing of locks of hairs. Citing the Old English derivation (**scortlog**, meaning short hair), he notes that Maundy Thursday was traditionally known for the "custom of shearing or shaving the beard" and deduces from this connection that Holmes was born on that day, but the exact day has now been disputed.[10] Surely we have no **urgency** to believe that the origin of the name related to the day on which he was born.

Is there anything new that can be added? I should like to add several ideas, which may have occurred to others but not in any of the material I have come across. The first is that even as Holmes refers to the "most abstruse cryptogram", so his first name can be understood that way, but not in terms of Conan Doyle's intent. (Cryptograms are cryptograms, it is said, regardless of intent.) The puzzle would here take the form of an anagram. If so, a simple transposition of the first letter to the end tells us that Sherlock was named after his mother's esteem for his curly hair; hence it meant "her locks". From a Freudian point of view, such a reading would hold, since a basic insight of the founder of psychoanalysis was that the child is attracted from infancy to the opposite sex. Shades of The Seven Per Cent Solution? That would perhaps explain why the adult Sherlock then had so little to do with women. Although he called Irene Adler "the woman", the real woman in his life was the one who gave birth to him. If this view seems a bit far-fetched, it is at least no more so than many other such source studies, and it is a truism that unconscious emotions and their reasons are different indeed from common sense. Elsewhere[11] I have studied the origin of the related name Shylock and have concluded that it too was a "homesy" word, having an English rather than a Hebrew origin, possibly one relating to recusant Richard Shacklock (since the Catholic redusants compared their plight to that of the Israelites). It is, in fact, more likely that Doyle would have heard of the recusant's name than Shakespeare would have, so I would not totally rule out a Shylock-Shacklock-Sherlock connection (a combination "lock"?). But, in any event, when a man's last name already connoted home territory (i.e., Holmes), we have all the more reason to suspect that his first name did too.[12]

In any case, if Sherlock connotes a "sure" thing (sure with a Scottish burr), than Watson by the same first syllable token connotes the everlasting questioner, the stooge, the man who does not know: "What?" (or is it "Wot"?). Yet now I am being psycholinguistic. Instead of "Is it Hoyle?" let us ask "Is it Doyle?".

NOTES

1. Stanley Mackenzie, review of Malcom Watson and Edward La Serre, **Sheerluck Jones**. London: Peter Schoffer, 1982, in **Baker Street MISCELLANEA**, No. 30, 1982, p.35.
2. I have disclosed the source of this tidbit in my critical essay "Sheerluck Holds Out? A Piece of Promiscuous Parody", submitted to **The Baker Street Journal** but unacknowledged for many months now.
3. The first "Homing in on Holmes" conference held by **Central State** and **Wright State Universities** in **November 1981**. The commentator was Chuck Dean.
4. Jon L. Lellenberg, "Sherlock Holmes in Parody and Pastiche, Part II. 1930-1981", **Baker Street Miscellanea**, No. 28, p.32. He also discusses on this page Robert L. Fish's parodies about Schlock Homes of Bagel Street.
5. I have discussed this view in my essay "'The Woman is Only the Woman, But a Well-Stacked Calabash is a Smoke': Ruminations on Sherlock and Shylock", submitted to **Calabash** but also for some time unacknowledged.
6. The **Quest for Sherlock Holmes: A Biographical Study of Arthur Conan Doyle**. BArnes and Noble, 1983, p. 116. For some reason this proposed etymology strongly appeals to my students. Donald A. Redmond, in his important **Sherlock Holmes: A Study in Sources**. McGill-Queen's University Press: Kingston and Montreal, 1982., cites Doyle's own modest claim that he got Sherlock's name from a bowler ("L'Envoi", p. 303). (The London Times, in

the review of Edwards by Julian Symons, cited Fielder's view that **Sherlock** was a "grafting of Doyle's original 'Sherrington' and a sudden "emergence in his undermind of the Jew Shylock'".
7. Patricia Craig, in the **TLS**, 24 December, 1982, p. 1414. She calls Edwards' book "a fairly eccentric pursuit". "Even Agatha Christie's Poirot never sparked off this obsessive ferreting on the part of his admirers." What she appears to overlook (deliberately or not) is that such obsession with minutiae is simply typical of Holmes' own methods.
8. The point was raised in Philip Gerber's article "Namen als Symbol" in **Neue Rundschau.** Frankfurt, 1972, pp. 499-513. Gerber also went extensively into the Sherlock-shylock connection, as has Leslie Fiedler. The essay was also in **Das Grosse Sherlock Holmes Buch**, which I have not seen.
9. "On the Birthday of Sherlock Holmes", **Baker Street Miscellanea**, No. 28, p.4. This was read at "Homing in on Holmes". (see note 3).
10. See Raymond L. Holly's response to Lauria, "April 5, 1894", **BSM**, No. 34, pp 19-22.
11. "A Key to the Name Shylock", **American Notes and Queries**, 5, 1966, pp. 52-54. The view that it came from the Hebrew (**cormorant**) is not cogent.
12. It so happens that an exact anagram of the name **Sherlock** is **Schlocker** (if we double the "c" as Shakespeare doubled the "n" in relating his Caliban to **cannibal**), but such a neologism may best be relegated to a footnote. More germanely, Dr. Gerber finds **Holmes** suggesting the British term for a small island, **holm** (which may then relate geographically to **loch** or **ford** suggestions in **Sherlock** and **Sherrinford**). Curiously, J.M. Gibson's paper "Shacklock to Sherlock" **(The Sherlock Holmes Journal**, Vol. XIV) enlists a cricket player called Shacklock again. But may not Doyle have been acquainted with the controversy over the etymology of **Shylock** in **The Gentleman's Magazine** and **Notes and Queries**?

Continued from page 50): devices as though they are proven. Some of the very best stories in the genre have supernatural elements--which are explained away rationally at the end. Jon says there's nothing wrong with writing a story "that addresses the question, what might happen if" psychic phenomena were real. I quite agree. But call it a ghost story, not a detective story or a mystery. Then people who like ghost stories will read and enjoy it, and people who like mysteries will find another mystery to read and not spend several hours reading what they think is a mystery only to be disappointed in the end when it turns out to be something else. When you mislabel a story, the reader has as much reason to be annoyed as would the purchaser of a bottle of beer which turns out to be filled with vinegar.

Jon states the problem too simply. When he says he doesn't think that "a position of total unqualified rejection of the supernatural is much more admirable than one of too-gullible acceptance," he seems to be saying that skeptics fall into that first category. I disagree. All a skeptic asks for is proof--straightforward, unambiguous, replicable proof, the same kind of proof that scientists and other rational men **(Continued on page 20)**

IT'S ABOUT CRIME by Marvin Lachman

NOTES ON RECENT READING

From the "Golden Age" of detective fiction come reprints of novels very dissimilar authors. Margery Allingham was a very sophisticated British author whose fans love her work and whose detractors call her "dull". Being in the former camp, I can wholeheartedly recommend **Flowers for the Judge** (1936) from Bantam ($2.95). it's one of the best Albert Campion novels and features his unforgettable ex-burglar valet, Magersfontein Lugg ("...he's got the courage of previous convictions..."). There's a great deal of talk (mostly clever) in **Flowers**, but enough action, detection, and atmosphere to make it totally satisfying. As she often did, Allingham makes marvelous use of London's pea-soup fogs. Another Bantam reprint is Allingham's **Dancers in Mourning** (1937) ($2.95), which is even more sophisticated, with its background of British Theatre and Noel Coward-type character. This is a book with some surprising revelations regarding the personal life of Campion. Both books have covers that are veddy British and very good examples of paperback art at its best. The covers are bonuses; the books themselves are worthwhile without them. No one would ever confuse Erle Stanley Gardner with Margery Allingham, and yet, he is just as essential to a mystery fan's well-balanced reading diet. **The Case of the Lame Canary** (1937) from Ballantine ($2.50) comes from the best period of the Mason books. Gardner has been dismissed by many as a hack writer, and I'll concede that he had some glaring weaknesses, like characterization and description. Ah, but his strengths--manipulation of physical clues, lightning-paced narrative, courtroom fireworks--more than compensate. **Canary** has all of these, and I found it to be sheer entertainment.

Ballantine's series of Cornell Woolrich reprints has reached ten, and two more are coming including the very scarce **Manhattan Love Song**. Most recently published is **Rear Window and Four Short Novels** ($2.95). The title novelette formed the basis for the Hitchcock film classic, and it's worth reading even if you've seen the movie. There's also "Three O'Clock", the choice of Francis M. Nevins, the Woolrich scholar, for "the most powerful suspense story he (or anyone else) ever wrote". I don't quite agree. it's great, but not the greatest. The book also contains the first book publication of "Post-Mortem" a short story that Woolrich wrote for the April 1940 issue of **Black Mask**, that long defunct, legendary pulp.

Still available from Ballantine is **Rendezvous in Black** (1948) ($2.95), the last and one of the best of the "black' novels from that very "noir" author, Woolrich. The plot of **Rendezvous** will not surprise you; it's actually the reverse of a previous Woolrich classic. Even the suspense, that hallmark of any Woolrich story, doesn't start building to its usual unbearable pitch until relatively late in the book. What makes **Rendezvous** one of his best is the way he uses words to wring the last ounce of poignancy out of death—and the life of its survivors. When a body is placed in an ambulance: "Something was being shoved into it. Something that no one had any use for...something to be thrown away.... He was still there. He didn't know where to go. he didn't have any place to go. In the whole world there was no place to go but this." Much of the reputation of Chandler and Ross Macdonald is based on their skilled use of metaphors. They also abused them. Woolrich was more sparing regarding these and probably had a better E.R.A. (Earned Respect Average). Here's a good example from **Rendezvous in Black**: "He plunged his fist into his opposite palm like a tormented baseball catcher."

Because his quality is so good, I'm glad that Robert Barnard is also prolific.. A special delight was **A Little Local Murder**, his second novel, published in Great Britain in 1976, reprinted here in 1983 by Scribners, and just issued by Dell at $2.95 as #70 in their Scene of the Crime series. This is a thoroughly modern book, yet its devastating picture of a British small town called "Twytching", it's firmly in the best tradition of Sayers, Allingham, Marsh, and Blake. Of you are looking to U.S. authors for comparison, try Charlotte MacLeod or Emma Lathen. If you like any of them, you'll probably like Barnard.

If Barnard has a weakness, it's his willingness to sacrifice almost everything, including fairness in characterization, for a laugh. A gossipy character is named "Mrs. Leaze" so she can, inevitably, be referred to a "Mrs. Sleaze". The book's only homosexual, Harold Thring, is hilariously, but snidely, depicted. The ending is imaginative, if a bit hard to accept. More believable is Barnard's bright sleuth, Inspector parrish who dismisses his assistant, saying, "Thank you, Dr. Watson. You may return to your practice". Parrish also says, "Eliminate the improbable and what you have left is the bloody impossible". Yet, for a basically humorous book, Barnard gets considerable surprise and human feeling into his murder.

No sophomore jinx for Jon L. Breen whose second mystery novel, **The Gathering Place** (Walker, $12.95), is just as entertaining as his first, **Listen For the Click**. This is a booklover's mystery, set in a used bookstore in the West Hollywood section of Los Angeles County, and almost every page contains some insight into book collecting or publishing. Readers of **84 Charing Cross Road** will love this. Breen is not only knowledgeable about books, he also knows Southern California, its reading habits, or lack thereof, and its mass transit system, or lack thereof. There are some things about **The Gathering Place** which are hard to swallow. Several are very minor, including a writer who can type 200 words per minute (!) and a newspaper called the **News-Canvas**(sic). Did some punch-drunk fighter proof-read this book? More importantly, the plot hinges on a difficult to accept gimmick, the ability of a young woman to automatically write the exact signatures of dead writers like Fitzgerald, Hemingway, and Gardner. The reader unable to suspend disbelief regarding ESP finds his confidence in the book undermined.

As in Breen's first novel, there is a surfeit of detectives here. I counted at least three, and there was some sleuthing, briefly, by a fourth. I like to see one detective per book, so that there can be greater reader identification. Still, this book is so interesting, fast moving, and readable that the sum outweighs the flaws in its parts, and I recommend it highly.

For fans of the Holmes-Watson and Wolfe-Archie byplay, there are few better series than the short stories Lillian de la Torre based on the real life team of Dr. Samuel Johnson and James Boswell. Boswell was, of course, the first great "Watson" of all time, though his diaries were not mysteries. However, his subject, the great 18th Century British lexicographer, Johnson, was so bright and perceptive, that is was inevitable that someone would turn him into a detective in fiction. De la Torre, a fine writer of plays and true crime, did the job in 1946, and eventually tow collections were published. Both of these, **Dr. Sam: Johnson, Detector** and **The Detections of Dr. Sam: Johnson** have been reprinted by International Polygonics (IP) in beautifully produced paperbacks at $5.00 each. These are fine collections with special appeal to detective fans who also like history. The cover art is also splendid, but that's typical of this publisher. There's also good news ahead since IP is gathering more of the Johnson-Boswell stories and will publish two more collections, both original.

Everyone talks about Philo Vance, but no one does anything about him--except Scribners--which has been republishing S.S. Van Dine. They've just published **The Scarab Murder Case** (1930), another especially well-made paperback ($4.50), making five of the Vance books in print, including **The Benson Murder Case** (1926) which, as the first as in the series, is a good place to start your reading.

Do not be deceived into thinking that Van Dine is only of historical interest as the creator of the eccentric, erudite sleuth who was the precursor of Ellery Queen. **The Benson Murder Case**, 58 years later, stands up surprisingly well. It's true that Vance can be annoying at times, with his foppish ways, phony speech, and snobbishness; and it's true that Ogden Nash once wrote "Philo Vance needs a kick in the pants", and so does his creator, for parading his knowledge with unnecessary footnotes. Yet, in spite of all this, I thoroughly enjoyed this book.

Why, You ask? Perhaps because of its leisurely pace, intricately plotted crime, and dated view of New York City, it is the perfect antidote for the worst aspects of the city in 1980s. It harkens back to a simpler time when one could believe that it was possible to solve problems by the application of mental processes, an idea about which we are no longer certain.

The Vance books were tremendous best-sellers in their day, which no doubt contributed to the popularity of Vance as a screen entity as well. At least ten actors have portrayed Vance at various times, including William Powell, Basil Rathbone, Warren William, Paul Lukas, Edmund Lowe, Wilfrid Hyde-White, Grant Richards, James Stephenson, William Wright, and Alan Curtis. I have my own clear choice for the ideal screen Philo Vance: Clifton Webb, who never played the role.

Though most of John Collier's **Fancies and Goodnights** does not qualify as mystery, enough of its contents are in our genre for Ellery Queen to have included it in Queen's Quorum. Of the fifty stories, ten are mysteries, and they include Collier's's best, "De Mortuis" and "Back for Christmas". A surprise mystery is the delightful and less well known "Night Youth Paris and the Moon" whose surprises I shall not disclose.

More often **Fancies and Goodnights** is fantasy, with stories about the devil and anthropomorphic animals, e.g. the flea in the very amusing "Gavin O'Leary". There are also stories that defy classification, with the common element being the quality of the writing and satirical view of human nature. "Special Delivery" is one of Collier's best in this area, one of several stories in which he uses a deserted department store after dark as the setting. You won't soon forget its unlikely hero, Albert Baker, "...he sat holding a tourniquet on his courage which had already begun to ebb away". That's they way to use a metaphor!

Sex is a strong element in these tales, at least two of which involve mate-swapping. Yet, Collier responded to the euphemistic requirements of his time (these were written between 1931 and 1951) with an inventiveness and subtlety that can still amuse and titillate the reader. As far as I can determine, Bantam last published a new edition of this book in 1961. Another edition is long overdue.

John Dickson Carr died in 1975. For almost a decade before his death, he was in poor health and limited his output to a monthly review column and the occasional historical mystery. What a joy it is, then, to have a new collection of Carr's work, radio plays from the 1940s and 1950s, **The Dead Sleep Lightly**, edited by Douglas G. Greene, from Doubleday at $11.95.

In addition to the plays we get a perceptive introduction from Greene, our leading Carrian scholar. In eleven pages we have a capsule biography of the author, sketches of his leading characters, a discourse on Carr's methods, and considerable detail regarding his experiences in writing mysteries for radio. Few were ever better at this, and the nine plays are a varied lot, including two in which Dr. Gideon Fell is featured.

Don't expect Carr at his **very** best. Radio is a different medium from the novel or short story, and the writer must spend precious time including material that was necessary for the listener but is non-essential to the reader. Thus, the characters are described a;almost solely in terms of their voices. There is not enough room for the clues needed to allow readers to compete with the author in arriving at a solution. Motivation, never a strong point with Carr, is weaker than usual here.

And yet, there is much to recommend this book to the reader willing to be transported back to a different era and to read a book with his or her **ears** as well as eyes. The plots are clever, and the atmosphere is well conveyed with descriptions of sound effects, especially Carr's ubiquitous thunderstorms. There isn't a bad play in the lot. The best, surprisingly, were not those about Fell. I preferred "The Devil's Saints" and "Death Has Four Faces", both impossible crime stories set in France.

The collection whets one's appetite for more, longer Carr. Fortunately, I still have a few of his books unread which I have been hoarding. The introduction also makes me want to read a full-length biography about this son of a U.S. Congressman who survived the bombings of the Blitz in London and crossed the submarine-infested Atlantic several times during World War II. He did so to return to his beloved adopted country, Great Britain, only to leave her in 1948 out of disenchantment with her socialist government. How about a biography, Professor Greene?

DEATH OF A MYSTERY WRITER

1. **Leonard Kantor** early in 1984 in New York City at age 59. Kantor's 1953 Broadway play, **Dead Pigeon**, was based on the questionable suicide of Abe Reles, a Murder Inc. figure. It was filmed in 1955 as **Tight Spot** with Ginger Rogers, Edward G. Robinson, and Brian Keith. Kantor also wrote mysteries for television, contributing scripts for **The Untouchables** and **Streets of San Francisco**.

2. **Oscar Schisgall** in April 1984 in New York City at age 83. He

had been a prolific writer of mystery short stories in both pulp and slick magazines beginning in 1921 when he sold his first story to **Street and Smith's Detective Story Magazine**. He specialized in the short-short story and published over 400 of these, both mystery and non-mystery, in magazines like **Colliers, American, This Week, Reader's Digest, Coronet, Cosmopolitan,** and **Liberty**. Two of his 1948 magazine stories were reprinted in **EQMM**, "The Suspect" in October 1950 and "The Way I Killed Him" in January 1954. He also published a collection of short stories as **baron Ixell, Crime Breaker** (1929), and a mystery novel, **The Devil's Daughter** (1932).

3. **Ernest R. Tidyman** on July 14, 1984 at age 56. He was in London where he had gone for a meeting regarding a film to be made in Europe. He was born in Cleveland and was a police reporter for the **Cleveland New**. He later worked for the **New York Post** and the **New York Times**. He is best known for his mystery novels about John Shaft, a tough black private detective, but he also wrote non-series crime novels. As a screen writer he wrote the screenplays for **Shaft** (1971), **The French Connection** (1972), for which he won an Oscar, and many crime movies and television programs.

DEATH OF A MYSTERY WRITER'S FRIEND

Lillian Hellman on June 30, 1984 at age 79 at Vineyard Haven, Massachusetts. I have no intention of denigrating Miss Hellman by the above title. She was a major American writer but did not write mysteries. Her place in our genre has been due to her long relationship with Dashiell Hammett. She provided many insights into Hammett in her three books of memoirs, **An Unfinished Woman, Pentimento,** and **Scoundrel Time**.

Hellman's fame was won with the 1934 play, **The Children's Hour** and continued through such successes as **The Little Foxes, Watch on the Rhine, Another Part of the Forest,** and **Toys in the Attic**. Controversy always followed her, beginning with her first success, a play with a lesbian theme. During the era of McCarthyism, she was called to testify before the House Un-American Activities Committee where she denied membership in the Communist Party, but unlike others at the time, she refused to testify about her associates.

Recently, she has been controversial in the area of mystery scholarship because of her refusal to help some biographers of Hammett, though she was very cooperative with Diane Johnson regarding her 1983 book, **Dashiell Hammett, A life**. Of even greater publicity was Hellman's feud with two well known "mainstream" writers, Diana Trilling and Mary McCarthy, both of whom questioned her honesty. At Hellman's death, there was pending a 2.25 million dollar libel suit against Mccarthy because of remarks made about Hellman in 1980 on the **Dick Cavett Show**.

DEATH OF A MOVIE DETECTIVE

William Powell on march 5, 1984 at age 91 in Palm Springs, California. he played two famous fictional detectives on the screen, starring as van Dine's Philo Vance four times and as Hammett's Nick Charles in six Thin Man films. His first screen role had been as a villain (not Moriarty) in the 1922 **Sherlock Holmes**, with John Barrymore.

Powell played in many other mystery films during his long film career, including **The Dragnet** (1928), **Jewel Robbery** (1932), **Private Detectives** (1933), and **Take One False Step** (1949).

REEL MURDERS

MOVIE REVIEWS by Walter Albert

CINEVENT 1984

My record for seeing the new summer releases has been dismal so far this year. I was almost literally dragged by visiting friends to see **Top Secret** but was pleasantly surprised by the film, and it was reported that I laughed a number of times during that amiable spoof of spy thrillers. Once Omar Sharif was disposed of (and that, fortunately, occurred very early in the film), the evening passed painlessly. I enjoyed the exuberant rock-and-roll numbers that generated a lot of good-natured jumping and hollering and I would be perfectly willing to sit through **Top Secret II** if the redoubtable polka-dot cow with the floppy books is given star billing. I can't remember finding a cow so appealing since I fell for that sensible, matronly Mrs. Wiggins in Walter L. Brooks' almost interminable series of children's books featuring Freddy the Pig (as a sometimes detective) and a barnyard menagerie of engaging complexion. This is also a film made by people who have watched a lot of films and can't resist making references to them from time to time. Not a bad way to spend a summer evening.

My ritual visit to **Indiana Jones and the Temple of Doom** was consecrated at the end of three days of almost non-stop movie-viewing at the annual Columbus, Ohio Cinebash. Star billing—the film festival's much heralded center-piece—was given to a 1935 version of H. Rider Haggard's erotic fantasy **She**. It was directed by Irving Pichel (who was also busy acting that year in **Dracula's Daughter** that year as Gloria Holden's pasty-faced valet) and the enigmatic Lancing Holden, with familiar names from **King Kong** (composer Max Steiner and producer Merian C. Cooper) providing much of the visual and aural interest in this uneven film. The stalwart hero, Leo Vincey, is played in a forthright fashion by Randolph Scott, while Nigel Bruce is made to look silly in the throw-away role of the blustering English side-kick. Helen Mack has the thankless job of trying to distract the male viewers from the attractions of the good-bad Ayesha, queen/goddess of the lost city of Kor, which has been transported from Haggard's African setting to an Asiatic ice-world which provides an excuse for the most striking set-up of the film: the discovery of a centuries-old European and a gigantic sabre-tooth tiger frozen into the ice outside the mountain entrance to the hidden city. Helen Gahagan, congresswoman and wife of actor Melvyn Douglas, played She with an effective mixture of icy imperturbabilty and melting languor. But her best moment had her still shrouded in the steamy mist to which she frequently retreated for mysterious purposes, intoning her lines in a voice that was strikingly similar to the voice of the evil, beautiful queen in the Disney **Snow**

White. And this affinity was compounded by a shifting facial image like that of the mirror image in the Queen's chambers a costume that was too similar to the costume for Disney's queen not to have been adapted by him. This film would, I am sure, be a popular addition to Saturday afternoon and late night TV schedules and it's surprising that it doesn't turn up more frequently.

If **She** satisfied our taste for romantic adventure, several films were of interest to the crime addict. The first film of the weekend was one that Marv Lachman reported on recently, Universal's **Lady on a Train**. This was a somewhat ill-fated attempt to create a sexier, more adult image for Deanna Durbin. She's a rich girl from California who sees a murder from the window of her train and spends the rest of the movie tracking down the victim and, then, the killer. Universal kept a number of good contract players busy trying to distract the audience from the fairly irritating Nancy Drewhistronics of star Durbin but the chief distinction of the film is probably the fine score by Miklos Rosza and the handsome photography. This is a classy production and it's never classier--and phonier--than in the carefully staged musical interludes, one of which accomplishes the not inconsiderable feat of eroticizing a performance of "Silent Night" by Durbin. The plot is devious and there are several boxes to be opened in this Chinese puzzle before the final revelation. Add a mystery writer with a tin ear for language, Edward Everett Horton looking puzzled at finding himself playing second-banana to Durbin, and Dan Duryea and Ralph Bellamy as candidates for unlikely suitors of the year. Neither one of them approaches his role with any conviction but Duryea displays an appealing off-hand, casual charm. The script is based on a story by Leslie Charteris.

A film that was scheduled for Sunday morning, a traditional low spot of the convention, especially so this year since many of were in the screening room from 8 p.m. to 2 a.m. the evening before, attracted a small audience but was, I found, one of the most engrossing films of the weekend. It was **The Passing of the Oklahoma Outlaw**, produced in 1915 by a real-life lawman, Bill Tilghman, and was provided by the American Film Institute in an incomplete print in the which the "story" was often difficult to follow. It presented, in an attempt, at a brutal and unglamorous realistic style, the pursuit and capture of the Doolin-Dalton gang. The landscape was wintry and bleak, and the action was a series of laconic scenes depicting the relationship of the outlaws, punctuated by flight, pursuit, and death. the primitive condition of the print actually worked to the advantage of the film since it gave it the appearance of a documentary, like a window opening onto a past composed of stiff images in a family album suddenly brought to life.

This film was followed by a 61-minute programmer from Columbia, **The Mark of the Whistler** (1944), directed by the thriller king of the pre-Roger Corman era, William Castle, and starring Richard Dix as a drifter who assumes another man's identity in order to claim a fortune. Where there is no plot to speak of in **The Passing of the Oklahoma Outlaw**, **The Mark of the Whistler** was all plot, based on a story by Cornell Woolrich that betrays his obsession with characters who are haunted by a past they are not in control of and that they do not fully understand. There is no one distinguishing quality in this film, which has the look of a 50s television suspense drama. Everything was directed to a single end: to trap the spectator in the web where the protagonist was caught, and to communicate a shared sense of uneasiness between the drifter and the spectator. The scheduling of the 1914 silent film and the 1944 sound melodrama was an intelligent one. They could not have been more different in their approach to the subject—the one concerned with the real, the other with the dramatically staged—but their vision of man's fate was not dissimilar.

I was on a real high much of the weekend and I will only mention some of the other films to give you an idea of the range of scheduling: the first feature-length film directed by Buster Keaton, **Three Ages** (1923), with an amorous Buster wooing and winning his girl in prehistoric times, ancient Rome, and the modern day, in the face of villainous Wallace Beery's opposition; George Stevens' **Talk of the Town** (Columbia, 1942) with Ronald Colman, Cary Grant and Jean Arthur at the top of their considerable form in a "screwball comedy with a message", as convicted anarchist/murderer Grant escapes and takes refuge in the house law professor Colman is renting for the summer from caretaker Arthur; Peter Lorre in one his most outrageous—and effective—roles as Doctor Gogol in karl Freund's strikingly directed **Mad Love** (MGM, 1935), a version of "The Hands of orlac" in which the hands of a murderer are grafted onto the wrists of a gifted musician with dismaying consequences; Alfred Hitchcock's **The Lodger** (1926), his first thriller, his first big success, and, not incidentally, the first film in which he made an on-screen appearance (or, as it turns out, two appearances), a film with the look of a Fritz Lang production, in particular his later "M". And there was, finally, the special treat of the weekend, a showing of James Whale's **The Kiss Before the Mirror** (Universal, 1933), with one of those fine performances Frank Morgan gave consistently before he was type-cast by MGM, acting with an intelligence and intensity that would undoubtedly surprise the fans of his 40s films. Here, he is a lawyer defending his best friend on a murder charge, accused of killing his wife at a lovers' tryst. Morgan has discovered that his own wife has a lover, and his defense of his friend (Paul Lukas) mirrors his own dilemma and the defense that might be mounted for him as he feels himself drawn toward a similar crime. The courtroom sequence is brilliantly directed and it has the most unsettling movie climax I've witnessed since Carrie rose suddenly out of her grave in Brian DePalma's contemporary shocker. And in the first 10 minutes of the film there is one of those stylized Whale landscapes that have haunted me from my first contact with with his **Bride of Frankenstein** in a movie trailer in the thirties.

As I left Columbus, supposedly sated with a surfeit of film watching, I cleverly arranged my exit so that I passed the only theater in Columbus showing **Indiana Jones and the Temple of Doom** in a 70-mm print and Dolby stereo sound. Yes, the thrills tumble along almost on top of each other; yes, the film is silly, gory and tasteless; and yes, I loved every minute of it. But, then, I have never been much of a supporter of the Legion for the Preservation of Decent, Tasteful Films That Even Gene Siskel Can Love.

VERDICTS Book Reviews

Edward Thorpe. **Chandlertown: The Los Angeles of Philip Marlowe.** St. Martin's Press, 1984, 112 pp., $12.95.

A strange little book, this one. The author is English and his aim is to describe for fellow Britons how the creator of Philip Marlowe portrayed L.A. and its suburbs and how the area has changed since Chandler made it his character's habitat. In thirteen brief chapters Thorpe breezes through various aspects of Chandler's life, his imaginative world and his city, including the way he viewed the rich and the poor, the way he used sex and violence, his attitudes towards women and homosexuals, and his interaction with Hollywood.

Thorpe's coverage however, rarely rises above the slipshod and superficial. He misdates at least one Chandler novel, frequently confuses the screenplays Chandler worked on with the Philip Marlowe movies scripted by others, ignores the most recent Chandler-based feature even though it was made in England (the 1978 remake of **The Big Sleep**), and wastes space with silly speculations on what Chandler or his character would think about events in the Sixties, Seventies and Eighties. Thorpe's writing style is serviceable if one overlooks gaffes like "superimposed on the townships, settlements, rancheros and plantations" and "what greater profit than that wielded by the...cinema industry". The final chapter of **Chandlertown**, which I suspect is the real reason for its existence, consists of promotional material for the Philip Marlowe TV series recently shoot in L.A. by London Weekend Television and broadcast here on HBO, but this chapter is just as superficial as the rest of the book. Even the 28 black-and-white photographs of house, autos and public buildings that graced the city during Chandler's heyday are rather ordinary.

The best part of **Chandlertown** is the photograph reproduced on the dust jacket, a striking shot of an L.A. intersection in the Thirties, hand-tinted in color for this reproduction. Everything else is negligible. With four years yet to go before the centennial of Chandler's birth, how many more quasi-books like this will we see? (Francis M. Nevins, Jr.) (The above review first appeared in the **St. Louis Globe-Democrat**.)

Georges Simenon. **Intimate Memoirs.** Harcourt, Brace, Jovanovich, 1984, 815 pp., $22.95.

He would have been happier, I think, if he'd been born a lion. To be totally at one with nature and the earth, to be surrounded by its enrapturing sights and sounds and smells, to adore and be adored by tawny, perfectly formed females in endless profusion and by the young they bear him—this for Georges Simenon would be paradise.

There's nothing new in this perception of the twentieth century's most successful novelist. Pick at random any of his more than 200 books, no matter whether it's one of his grim psychological studies or an investigation of Commissaire Jules Maigret, and you find yourself in the presence of the least intellectual and most sensuous of European writers. There are no clues and deductions in the Maigret stories and indeed hardly any plots: the great-hearted Inspector enters a milieu, mingles with its people and absorbs its atmosphere until he is so much at one with the environment that he senses the truth. In this respect Maigret's passion mirrors that of his creator, who has spent most of his eighty years on earth immersing himself into natural and human mileius beyond counting.

In 1972, just short of his seventieth year, Simenon gave up writing fiction. This huge volume of memoirs, written under almost unbearable emotional torment during 1980 and published in France a year later, is his testament. Although bursting with vivid scenes from his life, it's by no stretch of the imagination a full-dress autobiography. Rather it's an evocation of how he wants to be remembered by his children, his three sons, the ones who survived.

The catalyst for this outpouring of himself was the suicide of his only daughter, Marie-Jo, a gifted but deeply disturbed young woman who shot herself to death in 1978 at the age of twenty-five. Her death was the culmination of several years' open warfare on him by his estranged second wife, Marie-Jo's mother, who in interviews with European magazines has been flaying Simenon publicly as a heartless and sex-obsessed monster. If we believe his **Memoirs**—which portray him as an amiable, unaggressive and indeed passive person, except in his compulsive sex life much like Maigret himself—he chose not to dignify her lies with response until Marie-Jo's death and his discovery from her intimate diaries that in her early teens she had been sexually abused by her mother.

That devastating revelation was the catalyst for the **Memoirs**, an epic symphony of life as powerful as the masterworks of Bruckner and Mahler and Shostakovich. Simenon opens with the dark theme of Marie-Jo's death, then entrances us with hundreds of pages of lovely sensuous word-melodies drawn from his richly varied life. Youth in Belgium, early days as a journalist with the **Gazette de Liège**, move to Paris in 1922, marriage to an artist, turning out up to 80 pages a day of junk fiction for French newspapers and throwaway book publishers, long journeys through the glorious countryside, excursions along Europe's canals, the creation of Maigret in 1929 while moored at the Dutch port of Delfzijl, life on the grand scale during the Thirties, the coming of the war and the German occupation (which Simenon sat out as a simple farmer in the Vendee), the postwar move to the United States, the chance meeting in New York with the French-Canadian woman who was to become his second wife. It's with her entry into the story that the dark themes begin to sound again, muted at first, interwoven with the themes of his sexual passion for her and the beauty of Arizona deserts and New England winters. Then, after the return of the family to Europe, as she descends from mild insecurity through manic-depressive episodes to total paranoid schizophrenia compounded by alcoholism and a wild resolve to destroy her husband as a writer and a man, the darkness overpowers the paean-to-life motifs and we are in the world of a putrefying marriage something like the one he described in his late novel **The Cat** (1967). The circle begins to close as the first **noir** theme sounds again and Simenon's daughter kills herself. But the final notes are serene: she's at peace now, her ashes scattered in her father's garden, nurturing the birds and flowers. Marie-Jo's own writings, more than 150 pages of stories, letters, poems full of love and pain, form a sort of coda to the symphony.

But how much of this haunting, emotionally exhausting book are we to believe? Could Simenon possibly have had hundreds of long and short-term affairs during his first marriage without his then wife ever suspecting? How could a novelist so sensitive to character and atmosphere have been so blind to the problems of his second wife for so many years? Why does he feel the need to reiterate literally hundreds of times how deeply he loved his children? Could any human being have been such a giving and compassionate father as Simenon insists he was? Did he innocently contribute to his daughter's permanent sexual infatuation with him? If his second wife was the Darth Vader in skirts that this book paints her, why didn't he divorce her, or, if for some reason that was impossible, did he never consider the option so many men in his novels have taken: killing her? Readers whose critical faculties survive Simenon's almost more than human power with words are bound to ask these questions and dozens more. At this moment there are no answers. Some day, when Georges Simenon has returned to his beloved earth and objective biography becomes possible, we'll know more. For now we have his **Memoirs,** an impassioned self-portrait which, whatever its historical value, whatever the final judgement on its author, makes us see the profound truth of the maxim that underlies every Simenon novel: that it's a most difficult task to be a human being. (Francis M. Nevins, Jr.) (The above review first appeared in the **St Louis Globe-Democrat.)**

Jonathan Gash. **The Grail Tree.** Dell Scene of the Crime, 1982, $2.50.

Lovejoy's third adventure sets him on the trail of nothing less than the Holy Grail. It may take him a while to juggle several women and carry on for pages about this lovely piece of Irish glass, or that common-as-water pair of Satsumas vases, but much of it ties in at the end. A plot synopsis would be difficult due to the pleasant meanderings which build so much of Lovejoy's character. Suffice it to say that an old man has an old pewter cup that he believes is the Grail. Just as Lovejoy is halfway beginning to believe that the old man **may** have something worth looking at, the old man is killed when his houseboat explodes in the night. Lovejoy is certain it is murder, but the police say it is accident.

Unscrupulous, greedy, vicious, and sexist as he is, Lovejoy is, nevertheless, the hero. Readers like him and are on his side. Not in spite of what he is, but because he is so open about being a heel, and yet he's a sucker as far as antiques are concerned. A turn-about ending may leave Lovejoy with a partner for at least a few more adventures. Beyond that the other characters are rather thin and indistinguishable. But a fast-paced, suspenseful, action-filled finale helps atone for any blank spaces along the way. Anglophiles and lovers of series detectives will have a wonderful time. Everyone else will simply enjoy it. (Fred Dueren)

Leo Bruce. **Furious Old Woman.** Academy Chicago, 1983, Orig.1960, $4.95.

Leo Bruce's first eight books about Sergeant Beef and his aggravating, over-bearing chronicler Lionel Townsend, highly enjoyable and worth searching out. Then, for some reason, Bruce abandoned his beer-swilling, dart-throwing, ex-policeman for a new detective, Carolus Deene. Deene is independently wealthy, a victim of tragic widowhood and determined not to be a pompous dilettante who wastes his life. So he became a senior history Master at Queen's School in Newcastle, and decide to pursue his hobby of detection on in such free time as he could eke out. To use a trite, but once popular phrase, "Where's the Beef"?

Deene is not as bad as that may imply. But in **Furious Old Woman** he is a somewhat dull, plodding fellow. Bruce seems more interested in portraying a broad cast of characters in a small town dominated by bitter elderly females than he is in creating a suspenseful or fairly clued mystery. It's a kind of British stolidity at its most stolid.

For this case Deene is called in by elderly Mrs. Bobbin to find the villain who killed her sister and dumped the body in a grave prepared for someone else. Small town rivalries and church politics get a lot of discussion before the second death occurs. The plot and idea are actually rather striking. Perhaps Bruce's portrayal of rural England was just too realistic.

William G. Tapply. **Death at Charity's Point.** Scribner's, 1984, 213 pp., $12.95

William G. Tapply has constructed a mystery set in the domain recently thought to belong exclusively to Robert B. Parker; Greater Boston and its suburbs. Like Rick Boyer, Tapply is staking his own claim to New England, an area that is rapidly growing as a setting for novelized crime.

Death at Charity's Point starts slow, but picks up the pace soon after, cascading to a climax atop the point of land that juts out into the sea. The description and local color are well done, and the dialogue is certainly adequate for a first novel. Without giving away too much of the plot, suffice it to say that if you like a mystery with socio-political overtones, this is right up your alley. The main character, Brady Coyne, is an attorney with a specialized practice; handling the rich. He is engaged to find out why the studious, quiet George Gresham killed himself. The trail has many twists and curves, but Coyne gets to the solution (just barely in time!).

I enjoyed the book very much. I think there was more character development than in Parker's first in the Spenser series. That being the case, by the time Tapply reaches his sixth or seventh adventure, Brady Coyne could be one heck of a character in the mainstream of detective fiction. (Alan S. Mosier)

Isaac Asimov. **Banquets of the Black Widowers.** Doubleday, 1984, 216 pp., $13.95

The Black Widowers are in their forth outing in book form. This volume, made up of twelve tales (nine of which have appeared in **EQMM**), is not as satisfactory as some of the earlier volumes. I found the mysteries either too easy or too difficult to solve. Asimov's solutions are just too incredible to believe. Most of the stories's have endings (wherein Henry the waiter explains the solutions) that are just too hard to swallow, turning as the do, on the transposition of some very obscure fact.

Asimov has now written forty-eight of these stories, and this batch seems to suffer from his attempts to come up with more tricky problems for the "curious consumers" at the Milan Restaurant. Unlike Conan Doyle, Asimov is unable to sustain credibility in his plotting. He also uses his tales to espouse his own philosophy (particularly toward religious groups) in a manner that is somewhat arrogant. This comes out in the afterword of each tale. Although I began **Banquets** in a festive mood, I finished the twelve tales and left the table with a sour taste in my mouth. (Alan S. Mosier)

H.R.F. Keating. **The Sheriff of Bombay.** Doubleday, 1984, 192 pp., $11.95.

Inspector Ghote, the low-key and dogged sleuth of the Bombay C.I.D., has ventured into "the Cages", Bombay's seamier side of prostitution and pornography. Keating's portrait of Bombay is thrilling. You feel like putting on a white linen suit and stepping into the pages of the book. I like the way Keating writes. His books are well thought out and he has masterful pacing that helps lend that other-world feeling that pervades all of his Indian pieces.

But this time he doesn't play fair. He states in the first sentence that Ghote never had any doubts about who the killer was, but this is not true on two counts; one, he does indeed have doubts, and two, as it turns out, he doesn't know who the killer was. These quibbles aside, if you want something that keeps you entertained, that you won't be in a rush to finish, then H.R.F. Keating is just what you're looking for. (Alan S. Mosier)

Rick Boyer. **The Penny Ferry.** Houghton Mifflin, 1984, 254 pp., $13.95

Rick Boyer's Edgar winning oral surgeon, Charlie Adams, is back and up to his molars in a fifty year old mystery. Charlie, who was first introduced in **Billingsgate Shoal** in 1982, is as likable as that other New England sleuth, Spenser, but is better emotionally adjusted. His only problem is that he gets bored with his day to day existence as an oral surgeon. He has the time and money to do what he chooses, but he keeps getting involved in mysteries in the manner of Eric Ambler--innocent bystander drawn into the thick of skullduggery. Mysteries draw him like magnets.

This time he gets involved in a riveting mystery concerning the trial and executions of Sacco and Vanzetti in the 1920s. There is a good deal of mayhem and some amusing and well done sexual asides, but with one minor complaint I truly can recommend this mystery.

Boyer gives Adams one trait that I wish writers would lay to rest; gourmet cooking. Rex Stout did it first and best, then Parker and now Boyer have jumped onto the culinary bandwagon. I kept getting hungry. Can't someone come up with a detective that makes grilled cheese sandwiches and drinks Schlitz from the bottle? (Alan S. Mosier)

Gary Stewart. **The Tenth Virgin.** St. Martin's, 1983, 243 pp., $14.95

Gary Stewart is a director, an actor, a playwright, and, let's admit from the outset, one of my favorite colleagues at Indiana State University where he heads the Department of Theater. As it turns out, he's also an able novelist, and **The Tenth Virgin** is clear evidence of that fact. What a relief and what a pleasure to be able to say that I enjoyed the debut of Gabe Utley, a New York private eye who travels to Salt Lake City to undertake a case.

In his youth, Gabe loved Linda Peterson—or **maybe** he loved her—and when Linda suspects that her teenaged daughter, who has disappeared, is embroiled with Morman fundamentalists, who still practice polygamy and oppose many of the practices of the modern Church of Jesus Christ of Latter-Day Saints, Gabe cannot refuse to investigate. The case takes him deep into the facets of contemporary Utah life generally unknown to outsiders, just as it forces him onto areas of intra-church intrigue and into hidden details of the personal lives of a broad cast of characters.

In a sense, Gabe also takes the case to discover whether or not he can go home again, for he comes from Morman stock and was reared in Salt Lake City. As he measures his memories of the church against the facts he uncovers about the fundamentalists, as he measures his memories of Linda against her present distress and against the attractions of Mona McKinley, reporter for the **Deseret News**, Gabe is also measuring himself against the youngster he once was and the image of the man he hoped to become.

Yet another descendent of Sam Spade and Lew Archer, Gabe Utley is still very much a separate, individualized creation. So is **The Tenth Virgin**, though all conventions of the genre (including a hefty lacing of sex and violence) are observed. The setting and the Morman background are intriguing, enriching contributions to the novel's appeal, and they are handle well, thoroughly integrated into the plot. All these factors combine to make **The Tenth Virgin** a successful first novel. (Jane S. Bakerman)

Mary McMullen. **Until Death Do Us Part.** Doubleday, 1982, 182 pp., $11.95.

In **Until Death Do Us Part**, Mary McMullen's portrait of a successful businesswoman begins gruffly, turns grim, and ends up grisly. There's not much to like about Jane Frame (and that rhyming name doesn't help things any) who bullies her way to the top in the executive placement game and who **cannot** stand to lose—anything. When her ex-husband and current lover go head to head over a prime job and Frame's plans for that job are thwarted, she feels that her professional status is threatened, that her personal life is badly damaged, and that her self-image is in danger of shattering beyond repair. Frame and just about everyone else begins scheming; manipulation piles upon manipulation, and wickedness and deadliness flourish. Few characters in this novel can be trusted, and their motivations are telegraphed blatantly, but they are men and women of action, and act they do.

In usual McMullen style, the bitterness of the main plot is offset by the sweetness of subplots, most notably the growing attraction between two of Frame's employees, Dana Reeves and Nick Quinn. Despite the "secrets" in the pasts of these and various other characters, the outcome will surprise no one but will satisfy readers who enjoy the formula-modernized-on-the-surface kind of reading. McMullen does mean well, and this is pure escapist fiction, good for an evening of entertainment for McMullen and **Dallas** fans or for those who believe that assertiveness reaps disaster. (Jane S. Bakerman)

Liza Cody. **Bad Company**. Scribner's, 1982, 200 pp., $11.95.

Bad Company, Liza Cody's follow-up to **Dupe**, her first novel, continues the adventures of Anna Lee, the London private eye who is handy with tools, feisty, abrasive, and very good at her job. This adventure finds her pursuing her friendship with her neighbors, a kind of extended family; worrying about her car; and still working for the exploitive, cantankerous Mr. Brierly, head of the agency.

Assigned to watch young Claire Fourie whose parents have retained the firm, Anna learns something about Claire's friends as well, and when one, Verity Hewit, is kidnapped, Anna, on the scene, tries to stop the crime and is herself abducted. Much of the plot is devoted to the difficult, forced alliance which develops between the young women and to Anna's attempt to head off the worst effects kidnapping can have on its victims. Other members of the agency staff, meanwhile, are working hard and well at solving the crime and rescuing Anna and Verity.

This shift in focus between the relatively static situation in which Anna is caught and the action which her colleagues undertake while sometimes a bit awkward is also useful. It expands readers' understanding of a fuller cast of characters than were in **Dupe** and also allows for exploration not only of Anna's personality but also of the psychology of kidnapping, a theme given considerable attention in recent crime novels. All in all, **Bad Company** is an interesting novel which exploits a topic of current interest, furthers its developing series, and reaffirms readers' belief that Liza Cody writes well and is getting better. (Jane S. Bakerman)

Desmond Bagley. **Windfall**. Simon & Schuster, 1982.

In **Windfall**, Desmond Bagley takes his fans back to Africa, this time to Kenya, where a couple of good guys recruit a seemingly unlikely but effective staff and take on a troop of well-organized, efficient, deadly bad guys. Several staff members turn out to be other than they initially appear to be, as do, of course, the bad guys whose cover is inventive, exploitive, and fascinating. Bagley's recurring analysis of the evil which can be done in the name of progress is demonstrated here--but to say more about the scheme would spoil a very good yarn.

The good guys, Ben Hardin and Max Stafford, discover that their several talents (as well as their codes of conduct and beliefs) mesh together very successfully, and Bagley once again uses developing comradeship and professional respect as a kind of subplot to the crime/adventure interest. Though this device may be a shade formulaic in the Bagley canon, it's very satisfying because it offsets the grim overtones of the criminals' scheme and suggests that decent human beings can band together successfully on both the professional and personal levels. Both Stafford, head of the expanding Stafford Security Consultants of London, and Ben Hardin, formerly of the CIA and more recently an employee of Gunnarsson Associates, a firm which also handles industrial security—and a little industrial undercover work—are crack professional operatives; furthermore, they are operatives with heart and honor as well as guts and guile.

The mystery surrounding Adriaan Hendricks, a South African emigrant to the US, takes Stafford and Hardin to Nairobi and on to Ol Njorowa (called by British settlers Hell's Gate). As always, Bagley's sense of place is right on target; every detail is vivid, but the detail never intrudes upon the action. Also as always, Bagley makes his tried-and-tested themes and methods new once again, sadly, for the last time. **Windfall** is a very good crime/adventure story. (Jane S. Bakerman)

John McAleer. **Royal Decree.** Pontes Press, 1983, 80 pp., $6.50, softcover.

John McAleer has literally hundreds of hours of tape recorded conversations with Rex Stout. He has put some of the most interesting parts of those conversations into this book. Organized into four parts—Rex Stout on his Craft, Rex Stout on his Peers, Nero and Archie, and, The Wolfe Corpus—the book provides interesting insights into the man behind two of the best characters in the mystery field.

Limited to an edition of one thousand, a signed and numbered copy can be obtained for $6.50, postpaid, from John McAleer, 121 Follen Road, Lexington, Massachusetts, 02173.

A must for those who enjoy the Nero Wolfe saga. (Linda Toole)

Dennis Wheatley. **Herewith the Clues, The Fourth Dennis Wheatley Murder Mystery** planned by J.G. Links. Mayflower Books, 1982.

This is billed as "an exact reproduction of the best-selling 1930s original down to the last detail, including the actual clues". What we have here is not a book, but rather a dossier of a crime. Included are police reports, photographs, small envelopes holding bits of physical evidence, sheets on which to mark the readers' answers, and a sealed section enclosing the solution and reasons for it.

A gang of IRA terrorists and drug runners have their headquarters at the Milky Way Club, a nightspot managed by a Russian refugee, Serge Orloff. Scotland Yard has recruited him as a stool-pigeon, and a raid has been set up. The gang meets in a secret room behind the club proper, a room which is locked by Serge after each person enters, and unlocked to let the next in. When Serge is killed just before the raid, the police have to find out who was locked into the secret room and thence escaped into the street, and who was inside the club.

The players of this elaborate game, that is, we mystery fans, are told everything the police know. It is up to us to interpret the evidence and find the killer. It's not an easy game. The physical evidence is not always clear; photographs are not easy to read, and some of the evidence is ambiguous. Nevertheless, it's fun to try one's hand. It makes a full evening's entertainment, whether as a shared enterprise or as an alternative to a quiet evening with a book.

Verdicts (Maryell Cleary)

A.E. Van Vogt. **The Violent Man.** Avon, 1962, 316 pp.

The publisher's blurbs for this book by science fiction writer Van Vogt are misleading. The story supposedly comes "spiraling out of the same electrifying tradition that produces such books as **The Manchurian Candidate** and Ian Fleming's James Bond stories". Further, it is said to be "a Breath-taking Novel of War, Sex and Super Espionage". In reality it is much more sedate and philosophical than that. Set in 1957, several years after China became the People's Republic, it is the story of hardy hero Seal Ruxton in a Communist prison/indoctrination center.

The prisoners, a handful of Westerners and several thousand Chinese, are given two years to become Communists and prove it to their captors. Along with a library of communist literature and the opportunity to catch flies and do manual labor willingly, there are fatiguing indoctrination meetings and crude, brutal brainwashing techniques--all presided over by the authoritarian, psychotic commander of the prison, Major Mai Lin Yin. Ruxton is quite intransigent, and also intelligent. He has a psychological theory that he, along with Major Mai, Hitler, Lenin, and Ghengis Khan, have what he terms a "right" personality--that of a person who believes he is always right, a sort of combination of the authoritarian personality with that of the True Believer. Ruxton will never give in, and his personality and theory enable him to stand up to the brainwashing while appearing to do just the opposite. In the end, Ruxton is thus able to attempt to free the Western prisoners.

It sounds bizarre, and it is. But there is suspense, even though the plot involves many monologues on political philosophy, brainwashing and terrorism theory (hence **The Manchurian Candidate** reference), and a minimum of espionage proper. What the book really is, is a serious warning against the specifically Chinese brand of communism, and so belongs more in the tradition of Cold War Yellow Menace/Red Menace fiction, such as **The Manchurian Candidate** and later books like Oswald Wynd's **Death and the Red Flower** and **The Smile on the Face of the Tiger** by Douglas Hurd and Andrew Osmond. As if to confirm the urgency of his warning, Van Vogt includes an appendix with a 62 item bibliography on China and communism, including such works as **Das Kapital**, Chaing Kai-shek's **Soviet Russia in China**, Edward Hunter's **Brainwashing in China**, and even an Avon paperback, **Eastern Shame Girl**. Heavy going on theory, but recommended for a change of pace. (Greg Goode)

Lawrence Block. **Time to Murder and Create.** Jove, 1983, $2.95.

Lawrence Block's other great contemporary series--and who can forget Tanner, the thief/spy who could not sleep, who originally focused the world's eye on this inimitable writer?--is about Matt Scudder. Scudder is an amateur private eye and failed cop obviously paralleling Westlake's Mitch Tobin. So far as I know, the first of his adventures to be reprinted in paperback is **Time to Murder and Create**.

The title is the only weakness in the book. Scudder's honorable and conscience-weighted character is well-realized, as are the various minor characters, most of whom are not repeaters to be found in later Scudder outings. The hero's involvement in the mystery of who killed his blackmailer friend is convincingly set up, and for a very long time there seems little to choose between the three suspects.

Then, we are treated to two Wrong Suspect solutions, and finally, the real solution. Block is even clever enough to know that the reader couldn't be satisfied unless all the blackmail victims were forced in some way to suffer for the crimes they had been willing to pay to keep hidden. Ingenious is **always** the word for Block and nowhere is it more appropriate then in describing this book. Highly, highly recommended. (Jeff Banks)

John Katzenbach. **In the Heat of the Summer.** Ballantine, 1983, $3.50.

In the Heat of the Summer by John Katzenbach is a fine suspense story of the stalking of a Son of Sam type serial killer in Miami, and of the symbiotic relationship which grows between the killer and the reporter singled out by him for "exclusive" coverage and explanation of the murderer's program of mayhem.

Katzenbach is a Miami newspaperman, which gives him the proper background, and he is very good at helping the reader acquire a sense of place for the city and the various neighborhoods where the killer strikes, plus workaday scenes in the newspaper office.

The series of crimes forces a crisis in the newsman's love life (his live-in girlfriend goes home to Mama) and a review of his own past actions. The killer was (predictably) a disturbed Vietnam vet; the reporter a draft protester/evader. The book is, most of the time, a better "modern novel" in which the self-examination often pushes the murders out of the readers center of attention.

Yet it is not a failure at suspense. The rather ambiguous ending--is the killer dead or has he merely worked a clever substitution that will allow him to move to another area and resume killing people--works well to prolong the suspense even beyond the end of the book.

Recommended, with this reservation: it does have some contemporary scene/modern novel elements which certain readers may find disturbing. (Jeff Banks)

John Farris. **Sharp Practice.** Simon & Schuster, 1974.

Sharp Practice is a 1974 thriller that I just got around to reading. My reasons for delaying the pleasure are too involved to explain coherently, having to do with the writer's concentration on horror fiction when I was reading very little of it. Whatever added explanations might make my reasons seem justified, they represented a large error.

This is one of the best suspense novels I have read, full of psychological insights and autorial trickery. The focus is on a modern-day ripper-type killer; the reader will be well advised not to believe everything he thinks he's told. The British background of the first third seems well done; U.S. small college in the South background of most of the rest is very nearly perfect.

All of which is, of course, my way of saying **READ IT** as soon as you can, and mea culpa for waiting so long myself. (Jeff Banks)

Alpha Blair. **Through the Eyes of Evil.** Nordon Publications, 1981, $2.50.

Through the Eyes of Evil is a real sleeper, perhaps the finest suspense novel ever published by this now-defunct company. The cover blurb promises "a terrifying journey into the screaming jungle of a madman's mind", and for once the text backs it up.

The psychological insights seem all too frighteningly authentic, the pace of the story seems to accelerate beyond the point this reader thought possible. Fear for the safety of the convincing damsel in distress builds steadily as well.

The London setting and what the reader is shown of New Scotland Yard investigative procedures seems true to life. Like the Frankenstein monster in the original Karloff film, the psycho evokes sympathy to balance the fear.

The damsel is an American, Carina Worthington, on a vacation centered around the London theaters. Early on, she meets and falls for Sgt. Jonathan Claridge, who is helping investigate the murder she chance to witness. Meanwhile, the murderer, always presented through his interior monologue in an intensely intimate portrait, is stalking her to eliminate a potentially damning witness.

The fact that she is traveling with a vivacious friend, the reversal of the usual sort of central character's foil, makes Carina's timidity and vulnerability all the more convincing. Perhaps predictably, the course of love runs zigzag enough to give the killer his opportunity, and the book rushes to a climax, followed by one of the more memorable endings of recent suspense fiction.

Everything about this book seems right. Most highly recommended! (Jeff Banks)

Thomas Perry. **The Butcher's Boy.** Charter, 1983, $2.95.

Thomas Perry's **The Butcher's Boy** is a delightful hit-man story of suspense. You'll be fascinated with the inner workings of such a career, plus the gradual tightening of the rope of circumstance that deals the title character a satisfyingly bitter ending.

But the other point of view character--and the interweaving of the two narratives makes for a beautiful counterpoint in the story telling--is a federal officer on the hit-man's trail. Very mod in that this "hero" is a female. Her story will confirm everything you've ever imagined about governmental incompetence. Not that she is incompetent, just human enough to make an occasional mistake, but everyone of her associates seems to be.

Hair-breadth escapes for the killer, who soon finds himself a target of the Mafia, despite the fact he seems workmanlike, conscientious and happy in his work, alternate with misreadings of evidence by police agencies at every level and one missed opportunity after another to wind the case (and the book) up quickly.

The writing is superb throughout. Highly recommended. (Jeff Banks)

Robert Barnard. **School for Murder.** Scribner's, $12.95.

A devotion to puzzle plotting in the Agatha Christie tradition coupled with a wickedly satirical approach to character and setting have made Robert Barnard one of the most enjoyable writers to debut in the last decade. This time, he turns his jaundiced eye on Burleigh School, a distinctly third-rate English private educational institution. It is not to be confused with a Public School, which of course is the British term for the more exclusive and prestigious private schools. Headmaster Edward Crumwallis is an emptily pretentious bore whose stingy wife charges the faculty for sherry at the periodic staff functions. Most of the teachers are misfits of one kind or another, including a math master who talks like Elmer Fudd, a classics teacher who left a better school amid whispers of Lesbianism, an embittered failed artist, a young recent graduate praying for a job at a "real school" the next fall, and a 19-year general substitute who takes charge of the school's boarders for No Salary. All the characters—masters, wifes, lads, cops—are drawn with vicious economy. Most memorable is Hilary Frome, one of the most delightfully despicable of schoolboy villains. Hilary has the headmaster snowed to the extent that he has been appointed to the coveted post of head boy for the following year, but none of the other faculty are fooled. When murder strikes down the expected victim, the school's tenuous future is further threatened and Superintendent Michael Pumfrey carries out the police investigation.

Barnard does have a stunt ending, one of the less-often-seen (and, except in the hands of a master, most likely to disappoint) variations on the Least Suspected Person, but one that some readers will anticipate, partly because he plays so scrupulously fair with the reader, offering one very prominent clue to the truth and other supporting indicators. More significant than the puzzle plot is the biting commentary on education, much of it with application to other systems than the British. This author almost always tries to put a real sting in his closing sentence, and here he provides a beautiful irony for the finishing zinger. (Jon L. Breen) (The above review first appeared in **L.A. Federal Savings Quarterly,** Summer 1984.)

Evan Hunter. **Lizzie.** Arbor House, $16.95.

On August 4, 1892, Andrew and Abby Borden were found bloodily murdered in their Fall River, Massachusetts, home. Daughter Lizzie, accused of the crime, was aquitted by a jury but has generally been found guilty by posterity, the verdict of history being embodied in that persistent quatrain: "Lizzie Borden took an ax/And gave her mother forty whacks./When she saw what she had done/She gave her father forty-one." The Borden mystery has held the fascination of students of crime as firmly as any American murder case because it is equally fascinating with a guilty Lizzie or an innocent one. Both before and for many years after the crime, Lizzie led the life of a quiet, respectable New England spinster. If she did kill her father and stepmother that hot summer day, what could have driven her to it? But if she did not, who could have? The most popular secondary suspect has been the maid, Bridget Sullivan, accused in Edward D. Radin's famous revisionary version, **Lizzie Borden: The Untold Story** (1961).

Hunter focusses on a hitherto unexplored aspect of Lizzie's life: her tour of Europe in 1890 with three other young women. He alternates accounts of the trip, including quite a bit of intriguing detail about London and Paris as seen by American tourists of the time, with actual testimony from the Borden inquest and Lizzie's trial. He finishes with a thunderously effective recreation of the crime as he believes it might have happened. It would be unfair to reveal his theory here, but it may not be too much to say that the novel presents a basically sympathetic Lizzie and that his solution embodies some elements of earlier theories of the case.

In his afterword, Hunter provides what every "faction" writer ought to: an exact accounting of what is fact and what purely conjecture in his novel. (Jon L. Breen) (The above review appeared in **L.A. Federal Savings Quarterly**, Summer 1984.)

Ed McBain. **Lightning**. Arbor House, 1984.

The 87th Precinct saga has been running now for twenty-eight years, and the appearance of this thirty-seventh story brings Ed McBain within six volumes of John Creasey's record in the Inspector West series for the largest number of books about a single police detective squad.

Anybody who has read many of the 87th Precinct stories may feel some anxiety through much of this novel because of the way McBain keeps bringing in characters and devices he has not used in years, apparently getting everybody and everything on stage for a big finale. Our old friend the Deaf Man, for example, who has not been seen around for the past eleven years, seems through most of the story to be hovering just beyond the horizon. The uncouth Detective Ollie Weeks of the 83rd Precinct, once described as "a vast uncharted garbage dump", returns in **Lightning** after an absence of five years. Policewomen, who have never been prevalant in the Eighty-Seven, figure prominently in this one: there is not only an old-timer, Eileen Burke, who played an important role in **Ice** last year, but also the remarkable Annie Rawles of the Rape Squad, whose services are indispensable in the resolution of one of the mysteries. The use of visuals (literal reproductions of magazine mast-heads, calendars, and cut-out pictures), once a McBain trademark but almost abandoned during the past few years, re-appears with customary effectiveness. If, however, the reader feels any real apprehension that the curtain is about to be rung down, it is dispelled on the last page, in what is beyond question the most surprising ending of an 87th Precinct story to date.

The story-telling in **Lightning** is up to the usual high McBain quality. The chase-sequence, which has become a staple of suspense fiction of late, is handled with another McBain specialty, in the employment of converging action, with the narrative point of view switching back and forth between the police and the perpetrator. As usual, the most minor characters are never permitted to remain undeveloped, even when they are only off-stage voices. Another 87th Precinct landmark, the running gag, is maintained here with the appearance of a "rug" on the bald pate of Detective Meyer Meyer and the consequent opportunity for roguish comments by his colleagues and erratic reactions from civilians.

The detection is characterized by some highly absorbing accounts of the work of the police lab, which can deduce a world of information from a few human hairs and rope fibers. Incidentally, anybody who considers the hard-boiled mystery to be deficient in mental activity should read chapter 8 of **Lightning**, in which Detective Annie Rawles performs a neat job of analysis with a calendar, as pure an example of ratiocination as could be found in Ellery Queen. (George Dove)

William Campbell Gault. **Death in Donegal Bay**. Walker, 1984, 190 pp., $12.95.

In the posthumously published first chapters of his unfinished novel **The Poddle Springs Story**, Raymond Chandler permitted his proud and impecunious private eye Philip Marlowe to marry money. it was a double-barreled boner. Although Dashiell Hammett's **The Thin Man** shows that the king can break any rule and get away with it, experience teaches that to draw the PI as other than a loner. and a have-not goes against the grain of the genre.

William Campbell Gault, a writer for pulp mgazines since the late 1930s, won the Mystery Writers of America Edgar award for his first novel, **Don't Cry for Me** (1952), and then produced some of the best private eye books of the Fifties, many of them dealing with former Los Angeles Ram turned PI Brock Callahan. In the early Sixties Gault left mystery fiction to concentrate on a better-paying market, sports novels for young adults. A few years ago he and Callahan came back into the private-eye field, only it's a tamed and domesticated Callahan, enjoying the easy life on a legacy from a rich uncle, married to a lovely interior decorator, under the thumb of their jovial live-in housekeeper, taking cases only out of boredom. **Death in Donegal Bay** is the most recently published of these. An ex-con man who has also hit it rich asks Callahan to shadow his spectacular wife. She's been taking clandestine trips to the beach village of Donegal Bay where her former lover, a failed prizefighter, runs a fish restaurant and bar. Callahan passes on the case to a sort of apprentice PI, an eager kid whose office is his parents' garage. and before long both men are up to their private eyeballs in a stew of blackmail, counter blackmail, dope-running, family secrets and murder.

Like the chowder in that fish restaurant, which is made with canned clams, this book lacks too many of the private ingredients. The thin plot sprawls all over the landscape, the characters are over-abundant and ill-defined, the writing plain and flavorless. There's no sense of tension or menace, of people trapped in their own skins, of streets dark with more than night. There's hardly any action, except for Callahan commuting around to interview suspects and deliver fabric samples for his wife along the way. The interplay among Callahan's 1930s consciousness, his bourgeois Fifities lifestyle, and the public events of the late Seventies when the book was written is never even explored.

A quarter century ago, William Campbell Gault was one of the handful who kept the private eye novel on course, joining with others like Ross Macdonald and Thomas B. Dewey and William Ard in saying No to the all but irresistable influence of Mickey Spillane and his sadistic macho shamus Mike Hammer. Let's remember Gault for his fine books of the Fifties, and quickly forget a misfire like **Death in Donegal Bay**. (Francis M. Nevins, Jr.)

The Documents In the Case (Letters)

From Bob Adey, the English countryside: (A letter that has been lost in the files for quite some time. Sorry, Bob.)

...Two letters to comment on. William F. Deeck's because he lists among his superior novels two by one of my favorite authors, Joseph Harrington. Harrington wrote only three books, all top quality, and in my view probably the best police procedurals ever written--but very rarely do they get a mention, so all power to William Deeck's elbow.

Secondly, Melinda Reynold's Dick Francis checklist didn't include Francis' contribution to a round robin short story published in **Britains TV Times** (the one with details of the commercial channel programmes). Full details are: Chapter 1 of "The Diamonds are Forever Mystery" in **TV Times** for July 12, 1973. The other three chapters, all in the same issue, came from Gavin Lyall, Miles Tripp, and Christianna Brand.

From Jeff Banks, Nacogdoches, Texas:

The second issue under your editorship was another world-beater. (**My blushes, Watson**) I know you are going to keep up the good work; [**It's you all that are keeping up the good work, but thanks all the same.**] I'm ready to excuse you in advance if you fail to get the magazine back on schedule. And I'll bet most of the rest are too. [**Except the eminence grise.**]

But the main reason I'm writing is to inform you of a new market for mystery fiction.

Tales As Like As Not, Second Unit Productions, 623 Laird LAne, Lafayette, CA 94549, edited by Dale Hoover, is now open to Mystery fiction. Heretofore the magazine has published SF, Fantasy and Horror, all of which it will continue to buy. So this means just a few (I hope as many as three) mysteries will begin appearing soon in its quarterly issues.

With the end of **Black Cat** and then **Spiderweb**, we amateur mystery writers have had no place to start our careers. **Tales As Like As Not** should take up some of the slack. It is a semi-professional magazine, paying $5.00 for each story published, regardless of length.

The editor, to whom I've been selling Fantasy and SF, told me he is a **Hitchcock fan**. I take that to mean of the movies rather than the magazine. And it may provide a tip as to what sort of work those who need such a market may wish to begin their submissions with.

From Marv Lachman, Suffern, NY:
I agree with Bob Samioan about Art's review of the Darby book. While I am against censorship, I don't believe gutter language adds to either the content or class or **TMF**. [Art?—See below, Steve...]

I did, however, agree with Guy regarding the automatic writing as plot gimmick in an otherwise very interesting book, Jon Breen's **The Gathering Place**. I said the same in my review which was completed shortly before receiving this issue of **TMF**.

Doug Greene is about as qualified as anyone I know to do the kind of history of our field that he is contemplating. When I was younger and more ambitious, I had the same idea. I got hung up and never went beyond the tentative title: **The Mystery: A History**. Well, at least it rhymed.

From Art Scott, Livermore, California, direct-to-disk:
This is one hell of a way to save a stamp! As Steve may have mentioned elsewhere, I was dragooned into salvaging this issue from digital oblivion. Since I have the opportunity, I might as well reply to the comments regarding my outburst directed at Ken Darby.

When the review saw print here I don't believe it was noted that it was originally written for **DAPA-EM**—a much smaller audience, and one quite familiar with (and forgiving of) my occasional earthy outbursts. When Guy asked to run it, I thought of "cleaning it up" a bit, but didn't bother with a rewrite, figuring that he would exercise his editorial judgment and do so if he thought it appropriate for this readership.

Well, he ran it as written; so be it. Had I reworked it for **FANcier**, I probably would have excised the offending word. However, I would **not** have toned it down any! I still consider Darby's book to be a detestable appropriation of Rex Stout's creation; and since for me a book reflects to some considerable extent upon the character of the author, the **ad hominem** outburst was inevitable. Poor reviewing etiquette, I admit; but excellent therapy.

Having been thus chastised, I'll refrain from mentioning here some of the choice terms I laid on Steve regarding his skills as a computer operator. . .

From Mike Nevins, Universal City, Missouri:
I can offer Joe Christopher only an educated guess as to where that famous quote by Dorothy L. Sayers about John Dickson Carr comes from. Based purely on my hunch that it reads like someone who has not reviewed a Carr novel before, my guess is that the quote comes from her review of **The Mad Hatter Mystery**. And I second Joe's motion that Brownstone Books should consider doing a collection of her reviews from the London **Times**. (Also a volume of Dashiell Hammett's reviews from the New York **Post**.)

As Doug Greene suggests, I did try to interest Doubleday in following up the Carr radio play collection, **The Dead Sleep Lightly**, with a book of Ellery Queen radio plays edited by me. No luck. But I have edited a collection fo the best Queen short stories which is scheduled for publication by Beaufort Books in December.

From Doug Greene, Norfolk, Virginia:
    Joe R. Christopher is right: I should have given the source of the quotation from Dorothy L. Sayers which I included in **The Dead Sleep Lightly**. It's from **The Sunday Times**. 24th September, 1933—an article entitled "Mystery Out of the Ordinary" (actually a review of Carr's **Mad Hatter Mystery** and Sutherland's **Behind the Headlines**. Sayer's comments were frequently quoted in publishers' blurbs on Carr's books, and Carr later said it was Sayer's review which brought his books to public attention.

From Jon L. Breen, Fountain Valley, CA:
    I've always had a secret desire to be a controversial character and have wondered what it would be like to be attacked in print. So you can imagine how stimulating I found the diatribe from my friend Guy Townsend in your March/April issue.
    Of course, I realized that some readers wouldn't care for the insertion of a supernatural wlwment into a detective novel, and did in fact include an alternative natural explanation, as one reviewer (Bob Briney) has pointed out, but I'm surprised to find someone suggesting that **The Gathering Place** is intended to encourage a belief in psychic phenomena. I'd have thought it was obvious the novel was meant as an entertaining story rather than a true believer's polemic. (For an example of that kind of polemic, see Conan Doyle's **The Land of Mist**.) Whether or not I believe in automatic writing (I don't as it happens) is really irrelevant. I don't think it's necessary to believe a certain phenomenon really exists to want to write (or read) a story that addresses the question, what might happen if it did? As for which of my characters speak for me, none of them do necessarily. They speak for themselves. I am generally skeptical about psychic phenomena, and I believe skepticism is appropriate. But I try to maintain an open mind, and I don't think a position of total unqualified rejection of the supernatural is much more admirable than one of too-gullible acceptance. As for the **National Enquirer**, I have yet to open a copy, though I do read the headlines in the check-out line as most people do.
    These are matters of opinion, of course, and I won't belabor them. But what about the matter of fact that Guy challenges, my use of the word "scam"? According to Volume III of **A Supplement to the Oxford English Dictionary** (Clarendon Press, 1982), one definition of scam is "a story; a rumour; information". Interestingly, two of the several quotes the **OED** gives to illustrate the use of the word in this sense are from works of crime fiction, William P. McGivern's **Caprifoil** and Joseph Wambaugh's **The Blue Knight**.
    In answer to Joe Christopher's query, my guide to courtroom fiction is called **Novel Verdicts** and will be published later this year by Scarecrow Press. It covers some 420 titles, including the two I reviewed in **TMF**, though my remarks in the book take slightly different form.

From Guy M. Townsend, Madison, Indiana:
When I finished printing out this issue (8:3) I found that it was only forty-nine pages long, not fifty. It wasn't my fault this time--Steve only sent forty-nine. I really haven't time for loc's, but, since the last letter in "The Documents in the Case" was from Jon Breen, responding in part to my letter in the previous issue, I decided to cover up this white space with a little blather, so here I am.

I was rather surprised that Jon characterized my comments as an "attack" and a "diatribe." The word "attack" is susceptible to so many meanings and shades of meaning that I cannot quarrel with its use, but I really would like to deny that my comments constituted a diatribe. Falling back on my old Webster's Third (which, for all its faults, is still the best authority for contemporary American usage), I find three definitions for diatribe.

The first, which is characterized as **archaic**, is "a prolonged discourse or discussion." Well, the portion of my letter which dealt with Jon's book was just under a page in length, and whether that makes it "a prolonged discourse or discussion" is entirely a matter of opinion. One person's short may be another person's long. [I originally wrote: "What's short for one person may be long for another." Then I remembered that Jeff Banks will be reading this, so I rewrote it to forestall any anatomical comments from Nacogdoches.] Besides, that usage is, as the dictionary states, archaic, and I doubt that anyone today thinks of diatribes as being merely prolonged discourses or discussions.

The second definition comes in two parts: the first is "a bitter, abusive, and usu. lengthy speech or piece of writing"; the second is "bitter or abusive speech or writing." Throwing out the "usu. lengthy," which has been discussed above, the two parts are really the same, so the question is whether my comments were bitter and abusive. My first inclination was to deny categorically that they were bitter, then I decided that caution required me to look up the definition of **that** word. Well, my words were not "cruel and oppressive," or "sharp and resentful," or "intensely unfriendly," nor did they "[exhibit] intense animosity." So far, so good. But I suppose they could be said to have been "harshly reproachful," and no doubt they were "vehement, relentless, [and] determined." But never, never, never were they "designed to cause pain or anguish." It seems to be a toss-up as to whether my remarks were bitter, but I'd say they lacked the meanness and hostility that bitter usually conjures up. Well, then, were they abusive? Of course they were; friendly abuse is a bit of a trademark around here. Technically, then, I suppose this second definition could be stretched to fit my comments.

The third definition is "ironical or satirical criticism." Well, Jon, you got dead to rights, there. I'll plead guilty to the third count and throw myself on the mercy of the court on the first two.

(For a genuine, bottled-in-bond diatribe, see my review of Cooper-Clark's paradigm of self-congratulation in TMF 7:5.)

Regarding the word "scam," I bow to the authority of Volume III of **A Supplement to the Oxford English Dictionary**. Were I in the mood for another diatribe, I might make some bitter and abusive remarks on the subject of whether Volume III of **A Supplement to the Oxford English Dictionary** is a more reliable source of information about American usage than Webster's Third, but I'm trying to limit myself to one diatribe per novel.

But I stick to my guns on my main point--that a rational genre like the mystery is not the place to treat psychic and paranormal
(Continued on page 24)

www.ingramcontent.com/pod-product-compliance
Lightning Source LLC
Chambersburg PA
CBHW031435040426
42444CB00006B/822